LINDA DOESER

World Food
ITALY

THUNDER BAY
P·R·E·S·S
San Diego, California

Thunder Bay Press

An imprint of the Advantage Publishers Group

5880 Oberlin Drive, San Diego, CA 92121-4794

www.thunderbaybooks.com

All notations of errors or omissions should be addressed to Thunder Bay Press, Editorial Department, at the above address. All other correspondence (author inquiries, permissions) concerning the content of this book should be addressed to.

Parragon, Queen Street House,

4 Queen Street House,

4 Queen Street, Bath BA1 1HE

United Kingdom

ISBN: 1-59223-132-2

Library of Congress Cataloging-in-Publication Data available upon request.

Printed in Indonesia

1 2 3 4 5 07 06 05 04 03

contents

INTRODUCTION

10 It has often been said, with some justification, that the essence of Italian cooking can be summed up in two words: seasonal and regional. There is another, perhaps less precise factor that lies at the heart of this wonderful cuisine—the legendary Italian love of good things, including good food. Learning the skills of cooking starts at an early age, as recipes and techniques are handed down the generations, and so too does an appreciation of well-prepared meals, whether a plate of al dente pasta topped with a simple sauce of freshly picked, sun-ripened tomatoes, a slow-cooked, aromatic beef stew, or a perfect seafood risotto.

Italians are natural gourmets, almost from the day they are born, and this, combined with their sheer enthusiasm and exuberance, makes eating in Italy a magical experience. Italians truly appreciate their food, and little gives them greater pleasure than sharing it with friends and family. They perceive the rich harvests of the land and sea, rivers and lakes as gifts to be used and enjoyed to the fullest. No Tuscan would ever consider a low-fat alternative to what is probably the best olive oil produced anywhere; no Neapolitan will count the calories in a plate of pasta; and although Roman women are among the most elegant and sophisticated in the world, they will tackle a dish of *saltimbocca* with genuine relish and a hearty appetite.

Of course, it is an additional advantage that the Italian diet, like that of most Mediterranean countries, is one of the healthiest today. Vegetables and fruit play a leading role, and complex carbohydrates in the form of pasta, rice, cornmeal, and bread are integral to informal and formal meals. Olive oil, one of the staples of Italy's cuisine, is high in monounsaturated fat, which is thought to help lower blood cholesterol levels. Variety—both within the range of courses in a single meal and among the dishes served from season to season—is the key and also the classic route to a healthy diet. The occasional indulgence in cream, butter, Parmesan cheese, red meat, or any other of those ingredients that throw food faddists and health freaks into paroxysms of self-denial is simply a way of life for Italians and part of a natural balance.

cooking through the year

Italians respect their ingredients and insist on the best quality, so although modern transportation and refrigeration mean that they can buy artichokes or peaches all year round, they still prefer to use seasonal produce that, if possible, is locally grown. They remain firmly in touch with that special, now sometimes forgotten pleasure of tasting the new crop: tender young peas of early summer, luscious grapes in the fall, or the crisp bite of winter's fennel.

In provincial towns and villages, people shop daily for fresh produce in the markets and plan the day's menu around what looks, feels, and smells to be in peak condition. In major cities, fruit, vegetables, and fish are rarely bought much in advance, despite the pace and demands of city dwelling. Even when the season is right, if the particular specimens on sale are not of the highest quality or have yet to reach perfection, they are left on the stall and a different dish will be prepared for lunch or dinner. A shopping list is only the starting point, and numerous deviations from the original plan are a welcome delight. It is probably true to say that for Italians the choice of vegetables is the most crucial part of menu planning.

This emphasis on seasonal, locally sourced produce and uncompromising quality has had a lasting effect on the style of Italian cuisine. Simplicity is the essence, so that the flavor of ingredients is never masked by elaborate sauces, haphazard combinations, or flamboyant garnishes. Fish, for example, is frequently sprinkled with a few herbs and charbroiled before being served with just a splash of olive oil and a wedge of lemon to squeeze over it—but the fish is freshly caught, the herbs are straight from the garden, the olive oil is flavorful and aromatic, and the lemon has recently been picked while still warm from ripening in the sun. The lunchtime spaghetti may be served with no more than a plain tomato sauce—but the pasta dough was mixed and kneaded earlier in the morning, the tomatoes are only hours off the vine, and the whole dish is sprinkled with freshly grated Parmesan, produced by a jealously guarded, centuries-old tradition of cheese making.

regional diversity

Italy has only been a unified country, first a kingdom and then a republic, for fewer than 150 years. Until the mid-nineteenth century, it consisted of independent regions and city states, and in many ways these have never really disappeared. Italians

Gondolas on the Grand Canal in Venice

have a saying that there is no such thing as an Italian and prefer to think of themselves as Romans, Venetians, Tuscans, Neapolitans, Florentines, and so on. Each region inspires fierce patriotism in its sons and daughters, who take great pride in their local customs, architecture, history, scenery, traditions, and cuisine. Indeed, this local loyalty extends to individual towns and villages within the same region—a devotion known as *campanilismo* that sparks considerable rivalry.

One result of this powerful local allegiance is that Italian cooking remains more regional than anywhere else in Europe. The distinctive culinary styles are further emphasized by the ingrained habit of buying locally grown produce. This does not mean that the

despite the trade in ideas, Italian cooking remains firmly fixed in its distinctive regional roots

country's cuisine is locked in the past. Indeed, new dishes and variations of traditional recipes are continually developed, especially in cosmopolitan, sophisticated cities, such as Rome, Milan, Venice, and Bologna. Nevertheless, Italians have enormous respect for and a great love of their culinary traditions.

The most obvious culinary divide is between the north and south of the country and this exists partly as a result of geography and partly through historical and cultural inheritance. Dairy farming in the cooler, wetter north produces butter, cream, and cheese, which feature in the cooking in this part of Italy. Similarly, both rice and corn are widely cultivated, so risotto and cornmeal are staples in Piedmont, Lombardy, the Veneto, and Liguria. The south of Italy, on the other hand, is the home of pasta, olives, and olive oil, tomatoes, eggplants, and citrus fruits. At one time, this invisible culinary border was impenetrable, until the enterprising Tuscans started to open restaurants in the south and introduced their own specialities, using steak (*bistecca*), bean dishes, and their magnificent Chianti Classico. Other regions quickly followed and the north, in turn, learned of *mozzarella di bufala* and goat milk cheeses, pizza, and Marsala, the potent, fortified wine from Sicily.

However, despite the trade in ideas, Italian cooking remains firmly fixed in its distinctive regional roots. Of course, this does not mean that you will not find spaghetti in Milan or cured ham in Calabria, but

The Piazza del Campo in Sienna is a popular place for cafés and restaurants. Visitors can sit outdoors and enjoy good food and sunshine

14

To travel through Italy is to take a voyage of culinary exploration...each province has its own distinctive cooking style and repertoire of dishes

Italians are far more reluctant to relinquish their traditional, regional dishes than most other Europeans.

the regions

To travel through Italy is to take a voyage of culinary exploration. The north–south culinary divide is only part of the story, for each province has its own distinctive cooking style and repertoire of dishes—and, naturally, each considers itself the best.

In the most northerly provinces, the influence of Austria and the southern Tyrol is immediately apparent in the rich soups and substantial dumplings on offer, especially in Alto Adige. Rivers and lakes in Trentino are an abundant source of fish, and game is plentiful in the mountains. Simple meat, variety meats, and pasta dishes are prepared throughout the region and pot roasts are a speciality of Alto Adige.

In the northwest is Piedmont, at the foot of the Alps, yet it feels more like a mountain enclave itself. Its foggy falls are a time of pilgrimage for wealthy gastronomes from around the world to savor its wonderful white truffles. Their delicate aroma can perfume an entire room, and they are seldom more delicious than when grated raw over pasta or risotto. They are also traditionally cooked in a pasta sauce with butter, garlic, cream, and anchovies. Game, such as hare, is abundant and comforting meat stews and casseroles, almost always with cornmeal, are served during the cold winters. Beef in Barolo, one of Piedmont's best red wines, is a classic dish that can stand comparison with *boeuf bourguignon* and,

indeed, the region has strong links with neighboring France. This is also Italy's largest rice-growing region. Piedmont is known for *bagna cauda*, a hot, garlic and anchovy sauce for dipping vegetables. The region's main city, Turin, is renowned for its sweetmeats, cakes, and desserts, many of them based on the local hazelnuts. Piedmont's smallest Alpine neighbor, the Valle d'Aosta, is the home of fontina, a delicious melting cheese, which is often served in a similar way to a Swiss fondue.

Friuli in the northeast and the Veneto, the region around Venice, are famous for magnificent seafood and fabulous risottos. The deceptively simple *risi e bisi* (see page 102) is a Venetian speciality that opened the Doge's annual St. Mark's banquet. So too is a melt-in-the-mouth dish of calf's liver *in agrodolce*, a sweet-and-sour sauce made from wine and balsamic vinegars. Polenta is a staple here, usually served as an accompaniment to meat and fish dishes, but pasta is far less common. San Daniele in Friuli produces a cured ham that some consider to be even finer than the better-known prosciutto from Parma, and cotechino sausage is as much as speciality of the Veneto as it is of neighboring Emilia-Romagna. The region is not renowned for sweet dishes, but does specialize in unique, delicately flavored lemon cookies called *bacioli*.

Lombardy lies in the center of the northern regions and its culinary influences are equally mixed—French, Austrian, even Spanish, and Venetian. Its dairy produce is second to none, so butter is used in preference to olive oil, and pasta is invariably topped with a creamy sauce. However, it is in cheese making that Lombardy excels—Taleggio, Stracchino, mascarpone, ribiola, Grana Padano, and one of the

Right *Bernini's Colonnade, Rome*

Overleaf *Sunset over Florence. In the city, fresh, well-cooked food can always be enjoyed with a bottle of Chianti*

great cheeses, Gorgonzola, are all produced here. Like the Veneto, Lombardy claims to have invented risotto and, certainly, *risotto alla Milanese* (see page 98) is a world-famous dish. It is invariably served with that other classic from Milan, *osso bucco*, succulent veal shanks braised in wine and garnished with *gremolata*, a piquant mix of parsley, lemon rind, and garlic. Beef and veal are the most popular meats in this region, and it produces an air-cured beef equivalent of prosciutto, called *bresaola*. Pork is only slightly less common here, and pancetta, sausages, and salami all feature in Lombardy specialities. Sweet recipes include *panettone,* a Christmas bread from Milan, as well as *tiramisù,* based on local mascarpone cheese.

The coast of Liguria is renowned for its rich diversity of fish and seafood, and the interior of the region produces tasty seasoned, stuffed dishes. The ancient port of Genoa was a gateway for the spice trade, and this is reflected in Liguria's culinary heritage. However, Genoa is probably best known as the home of pesto, a mix of fresh basil, garlic, pine nuts, olive oil, and Parmesan cheese. The Genoese believe that they grow the best basil in the world and are said to take a locally grown supply of the herb with them when they travel. Basil and other fresh herbs are widely used in Ligurian cooking and flavor the local pasta dough.

Focaccia, that dimpled flat bread, is very popular in Liguria, served as an accompaniment or made into sandwiches. It is traditionally baked in a wood oven, plain or flavored with ham, cheese, olives, sun-dried tomatoes, onions, or herbs. Italian bakeries produce very large loaves, weighing several pounds, and sell it cut into more manageable pieces. Almost as popular in Liguria are gnocchi, small, melt-in-the-mouth dumplings that are poached in lightly salted boiling water and served drizzled with olive oil, tossed in

The Tower of Pisa, in Tuscany

grated Parmesan or in a creamy sauce. The tradition here, as in northern Italy as a whole, is to make them from mashed potatoes combined with a little flour, but gnocchi can also be made from semolina.

Emilia-Romagna, two rather different provinces united into a single administrative territory, is a gourmet's paradise. Not only does the architecture of its principal city, Bologna, date back to the Middle Ages, so too does its reputation as a gastronomic center. The region itself is an agricultural cornucopia—wheat, tomatoes, rice, corn, fruit, and vegetables are grown on the rich soils of the Po Valley, while cattle graze the grasslands and pigs are raised throughout the countryside. Emilia-Romagna is world-famous for three products in particular: prosciutto, Parmesan cheese, and balsamic vinegar, and it can also offer an extensive range of other specialities: cured meats, such as mortadella and salami, and stuffed pasta. The trademark dish of Bologna must be *tagliatelle alla Bolognese* (see page 70), with *fritto misto* a close second. *Bollito misto* (see page 122) is a speciality of Modena, home of the best balsamic vinegar, as is *zampone* (stuffed pig's feet), and the entire region boasts a wide choice of dishes made with beef, chicken, ham, and game, as well as magnificent fish and seafood.

There is a difference—historical and culinary—between Emilia and Romagna. Emilia has aristocratic, even royal connections. Parma was closely associated with Napoleon's second wife, and her chefs were responsible for the legacy of fine pastries in the region. Savory dishes are rich and subtle, sparing neither cream nor butter. Romagna, on the other hand, has a more peasant heritage and the dishes from this part of the region are robust and flavored generously with herbs, onion, and garlic. The Romagnols also favor olive oil rather than butter.

In central Italy, landlocked Umbria has no pretensions to gastronomy, but the superb quality

Emilia-Romagna is world famous for prosciutto, Parmesan cheese, and balsamic vinegar

of the ingredients, whether freshwater fish, pork, lamb, or game, amply justifies a simple approach to preparation and cooking. The local olive oil has a distinctive if subtle flavor, and it is put to good use in cooking and dressing dishes before serving. Black truffles grow in this cooler highland region and feature in local dishes during late fall and winter, when they are in season.

The neighboring Marches region on the Adriatic coast boasts a rather more sophisticated style of cooking than Umbria and is rightly famous for the quality of its charcuterie, especially cured pork and sausages. Pork is the most popular meat in the region, although game, especially wood pigeon, classically served with lentils, is a local speciality.

Tuscany has become one of Europe's prime holiday destinations, not only because of the clear blue skies, golden sunshine, rolling green hills, and charming, sun-baked villages, but also because of its truly marvelous food. Olive trees were first introduced to Tuscany by the ancient Greeks, and today the region produces what many claim to be the best olive oil in the world. The keynote of Tuscan cooking is simplicity—a few, perfect ingredients are combined to emphasize rather than disguise the flavors.

Vegetables grow abundantly in Tuscany's warm climate, and beans are almost synonymous with its cuisine. Indeed, neighboring regions have nicknamed Tuscans *i mangia fagioli*—the bean-eaters. *Ribollita*, a cabbage and bean soup thick enough to be called a stew, is probably Tuscany's most famous dish, but the region is also well known for the quality of its beef, pork, chicken, and wild boar. Fresh herbs play an

The red wine of Tuscany, Chianti Classico, enjoys a worldwide reputation to match its olive oil

essential role. *Pan scicco*, a dense loaf made from only flour, yeast, and water, is unique to the region and is often used to make bruschetta. Pecorino cheese originated in the area around the city of Sienna, which is also the home of the popular Christmas cake *panforte* (see page 242). Florence is credited with the invention of the melt-in-the-mouth dessert *zabaglione* (see page 239), and the red wine of Tuscany, Chianti Classico, enjoys a worldwide reputation to match its olive oil's.

Inevitably, the best of the regional cuisines gravitates toward Rome, capital of Italy and of the province of Lazio. Roman restaurants are among the best in Europe but, perhaps because of their clientele's sophisticated taste, the food preparation tends toward elegant simplicity. Even so, rich sauces and robust flavors abound throughout the region. Pasta and semolina gnocchi (here oven-baked rather than poached) are more popular than rice, and the local meat—lamb and veal in particular—is excellent. Rome's signature dish could be said to be *saltimbocca alla Romana* (see page 146), a subtly simple recipe for pan-fried veal scallops flavored with sage. Variety meats, especially stewed tripe, are also a speciality. Much of the food in Lazio is well seasoned and flavored with a wide variety of herbs.

Abruzzi and Molise are almost invariably bracketed together, although they no longer form a single administrative region. The food in these mountainous areas is very traditional and rural, based on locally produced cured meats, sausages, and cheeses. Lamb is the most popular meat, and the coastal areas feature an abundance of fish and seafood.

Although not unique to Abruzzi, the exceptionally hot peperoncino chili is widely grown here, known to the locals as *diavoletto*, little devil. A speciality of Lazio, west of Abruzzi, is *pasta all'arrabbiata* (see page 87), flavored with these hot little devils. When the chilies have been harvested, they are plaited and hung outside the farmhouses to dry in summer to provide "central heating" in winter dishes.

The Pugliese are known as *i mangia foglie*, the leaf-eaters, because of their legendary vegetable dishes. Puglia or Apulia, in the heel of Italy, also produces fruit, particularly figs and melons, olives, herbs, and superb mushrooms. Pasta is immensely popular and some shapes are unique to the region. The favorite meat of Puglia is lamb, either spit-roasted or stewed with fresh herbs, but the local veal is also magnificent. The Adriatic fishing port of Brindisi is the place to eat memorable seafood risottos and other specialities made with octopus, oysters, or mussels.

The Campania region marks another culinary frontier—that between fresh and dried pasta. The city of Naples first produced packaged dry pasta, rather than fresh egg pasta, back in the fifteenth century and the rest, as they say, is history. Naples has many other claims to fame, among them the invention of the pizza. Starting life as a humble slice of bread dough, topped with tomato paste and cheese, then baked, this versatile snack has conquered the world, and the choice of pizza toppings today is infinite.

Meat is a rarity in Campania, but its absence is more than adequately balanced by the abundance and variety of fish and seafood, especially sea bream, red snapper, squid, shrimp, and clams. Pasta with clams is an essentially Campanian combination and typically it is served in two forms—white sauce or tomato sauce—each with its own passionate devotees. Tomatoes are the quintessential Campanian vegetable

Lifestyles and traditions vary from region to region and from town to village

Visitors to a piazza enjoying a coffee break

and appear in almost every course, especially as a colorful and tasty sauce for pasta. One of the region's rare meat dishes, *bistecca alla pizzaiola* (see page 127), is less famous for its beef than it is for the sauce of tomatoes, garlic, and onions. The region also produces two major cheeses: mozzarella and provolone. Mozzarella is thought to have originated with the introduction of water buffalo from India in about A.D. 600, but history remains obstinately silent as to why these animals first appeared. Mozzarella, tomato, and basil salad originated on the tiny island of Capri, and on mainland Campania it is invariably called *insalata caprese*. Campanian desserts reflect a more sophisticated, cosmopolitan past and include

some superb pastries—among them lemon-filled profiteroles from Amalfi.

Sheep farming is the main occupation in the mountainous region of Basilicata in the arch of the "boot" of Italy, so sweet-flavored, succulent lamb features in the local cuisine, but so too do pork and game. Many fine local cheeses are also produced. The cured meats and salami of the region are often spiced with homegrown peperoncino chiles, which tend to be milder than those from Abruzzi. Freshwater fish, including eels, are abundant in the many lakes. Fruit and vegetables flourish, and robust soups keep out the winter chills. Pasta is a staple here.

Calabria is situated in the toe of Italy's boot and its climate is perfect for growing citrus fruits, olives, and an immense variety of vegetables. Pasta is a staple and is usually served with a robust vegetable sauce that may include eggplants, baby artichokes, or sweet bell peppers. Desserts are often based on locally grown almonds and sweetened with honey or include fresh fruit, particularly figs. Exotic mushrooms proliferate and flavor stews, sauces, and salads. Chicken and game, such as rabbit, are the main types of meat. Fish is often on the menu, with swordfish and tuna being great favorites. Pizza is popular, often with a seafood topping.

Sicily, the island football to Italy's boot, offers a cuisine that is quite different from any on the mainland. This partly stems from the fertile, volcanically enriched soils on the slopes of Mount Etna and, even more, from the island's multinational and multicultural heritage. Sicily has been an irresistible lure to invaders over the centuries—influenced by the Etruscans, Phoenicians, Carthaginians, Greeks, Romans, Arabs, Spanish, French, and Austrians, as well as, of course, by mainland Italians. Although Neapolitans will never concede defeat, there is a claim that pasta was introduced first to Sicily by the Arabs and spread from there to mainland Italy. Arabs also brought spices and candies and encouraged the raising of sheep and goats. Fish plays a starring role in Sicilian cooking, notably tiny anchovies, sea bass, sardines, swordfish, and tuna.

The island can be credited with being the first place to can tuna. Meat, whether lamb, kid, game, or chicken, tends to be kept for high days and holidays, but vegetables are plentiful: spinach, eggplants, artichokes, pumpkin and other squashes, bell peppers, peas, fava beans, garbanzo beans, and tomatoes are prepared in a variety of imaginative ways. *Caponata* (see page 54), eggplant in a sweet-and-sour sauce, is a Sicilian antipasto enjoyed far beyond the island's shores, and the local tomato paste is the most intensely concentrated of any made. Sicilian capers packed in salt are widely exported. Lemons are used in

both sweet and savory dishes, and oranges grow in abundance. Sicily produces the sweetest almonds in the world and these, together with the local thyme-flavored honey, feature in both desserts and candies. Beautifully molded marzipan fruits grace candy stores' windows like little works of art. Another Sicilian claim is the invention of ice cream—certainly their granitas, slushy water ices, are popular for cooling down in the island's hot summer. Other tempting sweet concoctions include *crostata di ricotta* (see page 232), *cassata alla Siciliana* (see page 248), doughnut-like *sfinci*, *zuppa inglese* (trifle), nougat, and amaretti.

Italy's other main island, Sardinia, is different again. The Sardinians have kept themselves apart, and their

Sicily has been an irresistible lure to invaders...Etruscans, Phoenicians, Carthaginians, Greeks, Romans, Arabs, Spanish, French, and Austrians as well as, of course...mainland Italians

way of life, customs, and cooking have remained very traditional. Surprisingly, fish and seafood do not play an especially popular role in the diet, although tuna, red snapper, sea bass, lobsters, and mussels are abundant. However, game, including wild boar, and variety meats are important and pigs and sheep are reared all over the island. Spit-roasted suckling pig could be described as the "national" dish, while roast lamb is invariably the choice for Easter Sunday. *Fregola*, tiny soup pasta shapes resembling couscous, are a speciality of Sardinia. Fruit grows well, despite the very dry summers. The island is smothered in

Mozzarella is perfect for melting, developing a stringy texture that seems to have been made for pizza toppings

mirto, myrtle, which perfumes the air and is used in all kinds of cooking and to flavor the local liqueur. Typical southerners, the Sardinians produce mouthwatering candies, cakes, and desserts, often sweetened with the local honey.

cheese

The ancient Greeks introduced the art of cheese making to Italy, the Romans improved the technique, and over the centuries the Italians have mastered it. The different regions produce a range of hard, semisoft, soft, and fresh cheeses from cow's, ewe's, goat's, and buffalo's milk.

The most famous of all Italian cheeses, Parmesan, is a hard cheese made from cow's milk that can be produced only in a zone around Parma that is tightly defined by law. Parmesan made within this registered area is stamped with the words Parmigiano Reggiano on the rind. The cheese is aged for a minimum of two years, sometimes much longer, to give it a crumbly texture and a pleasant, slightly salty flavor. Parmesan may be eaten on its own or with fresh fruit, but it is best known for grating over soups, pasta, polenta, and vegetables. Though ready-grated Parmesan can be bought, it is better bought in a single piece and kept wrapped in foil in the refrigerator to be freshly grated as required.

A similar, but less good-quality cheese, Grana Padano, is also made in the Po Valley. It is grainier in texture and has a sharper, saltier flavor. It can be used in the same way as Parmesan.

Pecorino is the generic term for all ewe's milk cheeses. It is a hard cheese with a salty, pungent flavor. The best are said to come from Rome and Sardinia. Look for *pecorino romano* and *pecorino sardo*. The former is usually matured for a period of about eighteen months. This gives it a stronger, sharper flavor than cheeses that are matured for only a few weeks. Pecorino can be used in much the same way as Parmesan for sprinkling over robust dishes that can match its strength. Store, wrapped in foil, in the refrigerator for up to a month.

Fontina, from the Valle d'Aosta in the Italian Alps, is made from unpasteurized cow's milk. It is a semihard cheese, with a high fat content, a mild, nutty flavor, and a creamy texture. It is delicious eaten on its own and excellent for cooking, as it melts well. It is the traditional choice for *fonduta*, the Italian equivalent of fondue.

Another high fat, semihard cheese is Taleggio, from Lombardy. It has a mild flavor with a salty tang. It melts well without becoming stringy, which makes it perfect for cooking, but it is equally delicious eaten on its own.

Gorgonzola can claim to be the king of Italy's blue cheeses, although its veining is more green than blue. It is a creamy cheese with a high fat content, and the flavor can range from piquant to very strong, but it should never be offensive nor its smell unpleasant. It originated in the village of Gorgonzola in Lombardy, where the cows rested on the long journey down from the mountains to their winter pastures. The village has long been subsumed by Milan, and the cheese is now made all over the region. Gorgonzola is wonderful eaten on its own and it is also excellent for cooking because the flavor mellows during heating. It is used in creamy pasta sauces, stirred into risottos or polenta, or as a filling for crêpes.

Dolcelatte is a mild form of Gorgonzola. Torta is a layered cheese made from Gorgonzola and mascarpone, which is exceptionally rich with a phenomenal fat content.

In the villas and farms of Italy, distinct regional produce and culinary traditions are proudly upheld

Mascarpone is a delicately flavored, fresh cream cheese from Lombardy. Far too rich to eat on its own, it is used like cream in both savory and sweet dishes, from pasta sauce to ice cream. It is best known in desserts, particularly *tiramisù* (see page 238).

Mozzarella may be even more widely used in Italian cooking than Parmesan. It is a soft curd cheese, made in layers, then shaped into balls and soaked in brine. The balls are packed in whey to keep them fresh and should be drained well before use. Mozzarella is perfect for melting, developing a stringy texture that seems to have been made for pizza toppings. Fresh mozzarella is also delicious sliced and served with tomatoes and basil (see *insalata tricolore* on page 220) or with sliced avocado in a salad. The best mozzarella is made from buffalo's milk—*mozzarella di bufala*—and is always worth buying in preference to the more common cow's milk version as it has a unique flavor. There is also a smoked mozzarella, which is a lovely golden color and something of an acquired taste. Little balls of mozzarella are called *bocconcini*, meaning "little mouthfuls." Use fresh mozzarella as soon after purchase as possible. If you need to keep it, store it unopened in the refrigerator for no more than two days.

Ricotta, meaning "recooked," is made by reheating the whey left over from the process of making hard

cheeses. It is a soft curd cheese with a relatively low fat content that may be made from cow's, ewe's, or even goat's milk. It is widely used in both savory and sweet dishes. It has a natural affinity with spinach, and this combination is used to fill pasta and crêpes. *Crostata di ricotta* (Ricotta Cheesecake) is

a delicious Sicilian speciality (see page 232). Use fresh ricotta on the day of purchase.

Ricotta salata is a hard, salted version of the cheese, made from the whey left over after making pecorino. It has a flaky texture and can be used like hard cheeses.

Provolone is a stretched curd cheese with a dense, smooth texture. It is made with cow's or buffalo's milk and various different rennets. There are mild (*dolce*) and piquant (*piccante*) varieties, the latter made with kid's rennet. The best are from Campania and Puglia, but it is made all over southern Italy, often with differing local names, and also in the Po Valley. It is used in pasta sauces and eaten on its own.

the italian meal

Whether you are dining in a noble *palazzo* or sharing supper in a farmhouse kitchen, all Italian meals take the same basic shape. The food may be more luxurious and the table more elegantly laid in one, but the care that has gone into the preparation and the enthusiasm with which the meal is eaten will be identical. The Italian love of food is legendary, matched only by a desire to share a meal with family and friends. Busy lives may have changed traditional social patterns, but it is a rare family that does not congregate around a huge table at least once a month for all the generations to eat, drink, talk, and enjoy themselves.

Any Italian meal, lunch or dinner, centers on two savory courses, which are of equal size and importance. These are known as the *primo* and *secondo*. In the evening the *primo* is usually soup, while at lunch it is more likely to be pasta, gnocchi, or risotto, depending on the region. This is usually followed by a meat or fish dish, served with a single vegetable. Salad may be served with the *secondo* or afterward. Dessert will generally be fresh fruit or perhaps cheese, unless the meal is a special one. On more formal occasions, an antipasto or appetizer may be served. This may be as simple as slices of salami and a bowl of olives or a more extensive selection of marinated vegetables or a terrine. Freshly baked bread is served with every meal and used, without restraint, for mopping up every last drop of the tasty sauces.

Freshly baked bread is served with every meal and used, without restraint, for mopping up every last drop of the tasty sauces

Wine and iced water are served with meals, although children may also have soft drinks. At the end of the meal, coffee, usually strong, black espresso, is drunk, perhaps with a liqueur, such as amaretto, grappa, nocino, or Strega, for the benefit of the digestion. If drinks are served before dinner, they might include an apéritif, such as Campari, vermouth, or Punt e Mes, perhaps topped off with soda and ice.

The Italian approach to meal planning is to choose courses that are complementary, with harmonious flavors. A seafood soup, for example, would normally be followed by a fish *secondo*, such as *filetti di sogliole alla pizzaiola* (see page 167). A robust pasta dish, on the other hand, might be followed by a full-flavored stew, such as *stufato alla Fiorentina* (see page 124), and a delicate risotto would probably precede chicken or veal, such as *saltimbocca alla Romana* (see page 146). Such careful menu planning takes time. Taking the trouble is natural enough when you are entertaining guests, but for many of us it can prove too much work for a midweek family supper. But you can still dine Italian style by making the *secondo* a lighter, vegetable dish, such as *melanzane e pomodori al forno* (see page 197). Plus there are a great number of Italian dishes that are quick and easy to prepare, making perfect snacks, such as *bruschetta* (see page 55).

Opposite *Cetara is a charming fishing village on the Amalfi coast, famous for its* alici *(similar to sardines) and tuna*

in the italian kitchen

Many, perhaps most, of the ingredients used by Italian cooks would have been familiar to our mothers and grandmothers: flour, butter—always unsalted in Italy—bacon, cream, potatoes, tomatoes, and onions. Others have become familiar in the course of the past twenty or thirty years: eggplants, bell peppers, mozzarella, Parmesan, salami, pasta, and even garlic. However, if you want to recreate the authentic flavor of Italy, do remember that it is not enough simply to follow the recipes; you must buy the freshest possible produce when it is in peak condition. Each section of this book introduces the important ingredients. First, though, a look at what to keep in stock.

pantry items

Perfect fresh ingredients, from vegetables to herbs, lie at the heart of Italian cuisine, but pantry items, such as olive oil and spices, are what give it true vitality. As with most items, you get what you pay for, so use the expensive ingredients wisely.

olive oil

Olive oil has a rich flavor because it is pressed directly from ripe fruit. There are a number of different qualities. Extra virgin olive oil is made from the first cold pressing—that is, without any other processing, such as heat treatment. The resulting oil is full of flavor with a very low acid content. It is the most expensive oil and the one to use for dressing salads or hot dishes, when flavor is paramount. Virgin olive oil comes from the second cold pressing and is only marginally more acidic. It is a wonderful all-purpose oil for cooking—apart from deep-frying. Oil that is simply labeled "pure" is refined and may have been heat-treated. This oil is much less expensive and can be used for cooking, but is no good at all for dressings.

Many regions produce olive oil, and the flavors can vary considerably. The best is said to come from Lucca in Tuscany, but it is worth tasting different oils to

Olive groves are a feature of many Italian landscapes

find the one you like most. Olive oil from other countries, including Spain, Greece, France, and more recently, New Zealand, may be of excellent quality but will not have that quintessentially Italian flavor.

Once opened, store olive oil in a cool dark place for no longer than 6 months.

vinegar

Given that Italy is the world's largest wine producer, it is not surprising that red and white wine vinegars are of very high quality. Always look for vinegar that has been fermented in oak casks, to ensure no trace of bitterness.

Balsamic vinegar is made in the area around Modena in Emilia-Romagna and is produced and matured—often for more than twenty years—with the same loving care as wine. It has a uniquely mellow, rich, sweet flavor. It is very expensive, but because it is so distinctive only a little is required to lift dressings, marinades, and sauces.

dried mushrooms

Porcini, also known as cèpes, are the king of mushrooms. Although they are at their most delicious when fresh, using dried porcini is an easy way to give an intense and aromatic mushroom flavor to sauces, stews, and casseroles, and to enliven cultivated mushrooms. Porcini are available from supermarkets and delicatessens, and they are expensive, but a little goes a long way. Don't be tempted to buy cheap packages, which may contain other, inferior mushrooms. All dried mushrooms must be rehydrated before use; remember to use the soaking liquid in your cooking.

truffles

Fresh truffles are an extravagance that is probably beyond most family budgets. Canned truffles are available, but the whole ones are still very expensive. Truffle pieces and peelings are more modestly priced and can add a special flavor to many dishes. A few drops of truffle oil is the most economical way to add a wonderful aroma to pasta sauces, risottos, and salads.

capers

These are the immature buds of a Mediterranean shrub, and are usually pickled in white wine vinegar or preserved in brine. Capers make a good addition to salads, crostini, and pizza toppings. Sicilian capers are packed in salt, which enhances their flavor. They should be rinsed and dried before use. Caper berries are the fruit of the same shrub. They are larger than capers and have long stalks. Serve them with predinner drinks or in salads.

dried chilies

Peperoncino chilies are added to many southern dishes. Italian delicatessens stock hot, Italian dried chilies, but other varieties or red pepper flakes may be used if you can't take the heat.

saffron

The most expensive spice in the world comes from the dried stigmas of a type of crocus. In Italy, it is used to color and flavor dishes, from *risotto alla Milanese* to fish and seafood sauces. The threads are crumbled into the cooking liquid or soaked in a little stock or water then added to the dish with the soaking liquid. Saffron powder is available but may be adulterated with the less pungent safflower.

fennel seeds

This sweet, licorice-flavored spice is a popular flavoring for seafood stews and is sprinkled on broiled fish. The seeds are often sprinkled over bread dough before baking and feature in the Florentine *finocchiona* salami.

SOUPS &
ANTIPASTI

32 Italian cooks may value tradition, but this does not prevent them from being wonderfully creative. Not only does virtually every region boast its own version of such familiar favorites as minestrone and bruschetta, so does almost every family. The soups and appetizers in this book are authentically Italian, but they are not and cannot be definitive, so feel free to experiment.

In Italy, soup is usually served as the *primo* at dinner and is regarded as being equally as important as the meat or fish *secondo* that follows, not merely a preliminary to the star attraction. Consequently, traditional Italian soups are not simply packed with flavor but are often quite substantial. Vegetables predominate, whether beans in Tuscany, greens in Puglia, or tomatoes in Campania. The best-known Italian vegetable soup has to be minestrone—*minestra* simply means soup. There are probably as many versions of the recipe as there are cooks in the country, and it can be prepared with whatever vegetables are in season, providing no single flavor dominates and the combination is in balance. Depending on the region, tiny soup pasta or rice is added toward the end of the cooking time and, in the case of the Genoese version, pesto is stirred in to serve. Meat features far less frequently in Italian soups, except in the case of clear broths, when a good-quality beef consommé forms the base. Fish and seafood, on the other hand, are used in profusion in lavish, colorful soups that are often so filling that they could more properly be called stews. It is always worth making Italian soups in large quantities, as many improve with keeping and virtually all of them freeze well. Add any rice or pasta when reheating.

Served before the meal, antipasti provide a wonderful opportunity for creativity. They are always tasty, light, appetizing, and visually appealing, mainly based on cured meats, vegetables, seafood, and salads. Antipasti are often cold dishes and may be as simple as a platter of salami, served with olives and, perhaps, fresh fruit, such as melon or figs. Italy's superb cured ham, prosciutto, is also classically served with fruit, but pairs well with strongly flavored salad vegetables, such as arugula, and nothing could be simpler or more impressive than *carpaccio* (see page 46), thinly sliced fillet of beef marinated in lemon juice and extra virgin olive oil. Marinated vegetables, such as bell peppers, mushrooms, and olives, are a popular antipasto, as their flavors are complementary and they look so tempting. Stuffed vegetables, usually served lukewarm or at room temperature to

Above *A typical old hilltop town where local culinary traditions are preserved as part of its heritage*

Overleaf *In the heart of the agricultural region of Tuscany lie olive groves and vineyards. Wheat is cultivated and vegetables grow in abundance in the warm climate*

bring out their full flavor, are another good choice. The range is varied, including not just the obvious cup-shaped bell peppers and tomatoes, but also eggplants, which are a Ligurian speciality, and artichokes, which make up a classic Roman dish.

Italians are said to eat more bread than any other nation, so it is hardly surprising that tasty toasted canapés are favorites for antipasti. The simplest is *fettunta*, the name for toasted bread rubbed with garlic, drizzled with olive oil, and sprinkled with sea salt. With a topping of cheese, tomatoes, olives, anchovies, or pesto, *fettunta* becomes *bruschetta*. *Crostini* are similar and may be made with a bread or a cornmeal base. Mozzarella cheese is a natural companion for toast, as it melts so appealingly. A delicious Roman antipasto consists of stacks of small toast squares, sliced mozzarella, sliced tomato, and fresh basil leaves held together with skewers, drizzled with olive oil, and then baked for about ten minutes in a very hot oven. Naples offers *mozzarella in carrozza* (see page 58)—literally "mozzarella in carriages." In this recipe, cheese and salami sandwiches are coated in an egg mixture and deep-fried until golden. They are served with a tomato, onion, and garlic sauce—a dish substantial enough to make a summer lunch.

Fettunta, the name for toasted bread rubbed with garlic, drizzled with olive oil, and sprinkled with sea salt

36 # genoese vegetable soup
minestrone alla genovese

This classic vegetable soup is served with an equally classic pesto sauce that originated in the Ligurian port of Genoa. It makes a wonderful first course—primo—for an informal dinner with family and friends.

SERVES 8

2 onions, sliced

2 carrots, diced

2 celery stalks, sliced

2 potatoes, diced

³/₄ cup green beans, cut into 1-inch lengths

1 cup peas, thawed if using frozen

4¹/₂ cups fresh spinach leaves, coarse stalks
   removed, shredded

2 zucchini, diced

8 oz. Italian plum tomatoes, peeled,* seeded, and diced

3 garlic cloves, sliced thinly

4 tbsp. extra virgin olive oil

8 cups vegetable or chicken stock

salt and pepper

5 oz. dried stellete or other soup pasta

freshly grated Parmesan cheese, to serve

for the pesto

4 tbsp. fresh basil leaves

1 tbsp. pine nuts

1 garlic clove

salt

¹/₄ cup freshly grated Parmesan cheese

3 tbsp. extra virgin olive oil

1 Put the onions, carrots, celery, potatoes, beans, peas, spinach, zucchini, tomatoes, and garlic in a large, heavy-bottom pan, pour in the olive oil and stock, and bring to a boil over medium-low heat. Reduce the heat and let simmer gently for about 1¹/₂ hours.

2 Meanwhile, make the pesto. Put the basil, pine nuts, garlic, and a pinch of salt into a mortar and pound to a paste with a pestle. Transfer to a bowl and gradually work in the Parmesan with a wooden spoon, followed by the olive oil to make a thick, creamy sauce. Cover with plastic wrap and set aside in the refrigerator until required.

3 Season the soup to taste with salt and pepper and add the pasta. Cook for an additional 8–10 minutes, until the pasta is tender but still firm to the bite. The soup should be very thick. Stir in half the pesto, remove the pan from the heat and set aside to rest for 4 minutes. Taste and adjust the seasoning, adding more salt, pepper, and pesto if necessary. (Any leftover pesto may be stored in a screw-top jar in the refrigerator for up to 2 weeks.) Ladle into warmed bowls and serve immediately. Pass around the freshly grated Parmesan cheese separately.

*cook's tip

To peel tomatoes, cut a cross in the base of each and place in a bowl. Cover with boiling water and let stand for 30–45 seconds. Drain and plunge into cold water, then the skins will slide off easily.

38 # fresh tomato soup
zuppa di pomodori

SERVES 4

1 tbsp. olive oil

1 lb. 7 oz. plum tomatoes

1 onion, cut into quarters

1 garlic clove, sliced thinly

1 celery stalk, chopped coarsely

generous 2 cups chicken stock

2 oz. dried anellini or other soup pasta

salt and pepper

fresh flatleaf parsley, chopped, to garnish

Make this refreshing soup in midsummer when sun-ripened tomatoes have maximum sweetness and flavor.

1 Pour the olive oil into a large, heavy-bottom pan and add the tomatoes, onion, garlic, and celery. Cover and cook over low heat for 45 minutes, occasionally shaking the pan gently, until the mixture is pulpy.

2 Transfer the mixture to a food processor or blender and process to a smooth purée. Push the purée through a strainer into a clean pan.

3 Add the stock and bring to a boil. Add the pasta, bring back to a boil, and cook for 8–10 minutes, until the pasta is tender but still firm to the bite. Season to taste with salt and pepper. Ladle into warmed bowls, sprinkle with the parsley, and serve immediately.

white bean soup
zuppa di fagioli

Beans feature widely in Tuscan cuisine. This smooth, comforting soup, in which beans are simmered for 2 hours, is very simple to make. Garlic and parsley, stirred in just before serving, complement the flavor, and a drizzle of olive oil adds the final touch.

SERVES 4

1 cup dried cannellini beans, covered and soaked overnight in cold water

7 cups chicken or vegetable stock

4 oz. dried corallini, conchigliette piccole, or other soup pasta

6 tbsp. olive oil

2 garlic cloves, chopped finely

4 tbsp. chopped fresh flat-leaf parsley

salt and pepper

1 Drain the soaked beans and place them in a large, heavy-bottom pan. Add the stock and bring to a boil. Partially cover the pan, reduce the heat, and let simmer for 2 hours, until tender.

2 Transfer about half the beans and a little of the stock to a food processor or blender and process to a smooth purée. Return the purée to the pan and stir well to mix. Bring the soup back to a boil.

3 Add the pasta to the soup, bring back to a boil and cook for 10 minutes, until tender.

4 Meanwhile, heat 4 tablespoons of the olive oil in a small pan. Add the garlic and cook over low heat, stirring frequently, for 4–5 minutes, until golden. Stir the garlic into the soup and add the parsley. Season to taste with salt and pepper and ladle into warmed soup bowls. Drizzle with the remaining olive oil and serve immediately.

variation

Substitute cranberry beans for the cannellini and cook for about 1½ hours in step 1.

beef soup with eggs
zuppa pavese

40

Good-quality, homemade beef consommé is essential for this unusual soup. It is best to make it 24 hours in advance so that you can remove every trace of fat from the surface of the consommé.

SERVES 4

for the consommé

1 lb. 2 oz. beef marrow bones, sawn into 3-inch pieces

12 oz. stewing beef, in 1 piece

6 cups water

4 cloves

2 onions, halved

2 celery stalks, chopped coarsely

8 peppercorns

1 bouquet garni

2 oz. unsalted butter

4 slices fresh white bread

1 cup freshly grated Parmesan cheese

4 eggs

salt and pepper

1 First, make the consommé. Place the bones in a large, heavy-bottom pan with the stewing beef on top. Add the water and bring to a boil over low heat, skimming off all the scum that rises to the surface. Pierce a clove into each onion half and add to the pan with the celery, peppercorns, and bouquet garni. Partially cover and let simmer very gently for 3 hours. Remove the meat and let simmer for an additional hour.

2 Strain the consommé into a bowl and set aside to cool. When completely cool, let chill in the refrigerator for at least 6 hours, preferably overnight. Carefully remove and discard the layer of fat that has formed on the surface. Return the consommé to a clean pan and heat until almost boiling.

3 When you are ready to serve, melt the butter in a heavy-bottom skillet. Add the bread, 1 slice at a time if necessary, and cook over medium heat until crisp and golden on both sides. Remove from the skillet and place one each in the base of 4 warmed soup bowls.

4 Sprinkle half the Parmesan over the fried bread. Carefully break an egg* over each slice of fried bread, keeping the yolks whole. Season to taste with salt and pepper and sprinkle with the remaining Parmesan. Carefully ladle the hot consommé into the soup bowls and serve immediately.

*cook's tip

If you prefer, you could lightly poach the eggs before adding them to the bowls.

seafood soup

zuppa di pesce

Full of delicious Mediterranean flavors, this soup is less heavy and much easier to make than its Provençal cousin bouillabaisse.

SERVES 4

4 tbsp. olive oil

1 garlic clove, sliced

2 tbsp. chopped fresh flat-leaf parsley

1 dried red chili, whole

7 oz. canned plum tomatoes, chopped

1 cod or haddock head

$^1/_2$ cup dry white wine

$3^1/_2$ cups boiling water

salt

1 lb. angler fish fillet

10 oz. live mussels

1 lb. uncooked shrimp

salt and pepper

4 slices sfilatino or French bread,

each $^3/_4$-inch thick

1 Heat half the olive oil in a large, heavy-bottom pan. Add the garlic, half the parsley, and the chili and cook over low heat, stirring occasionally, for 3 minutes, until the garlic starts to color. Add the tomatoes, fish head, and wine and continue to cook until almost all the liquid has gone. Add the boiling water, season with salt, and let simmer for 20 minutes.

2 Meanwhile, remove the gray membrane from the angler fish and cut the flesh into bite-size pieces. Scrub the mussels under cold running water and tug off the beards. Discard any mussels with broken or damaged shells and those that do not shut immediately when sharply tapped. Shell the shrimp, cut a slit along the back of each, and remove and discard the dark vein.

3 Add the angler fish and mussels to the pan and let simmer for 4–5 minutes. Add the shrimp and let simmer for an additional 2–3 minutes, until they have changed color.

4 Remove and discard the fish head* and the chili. Remove any mussels that have not opened. Add the remaining olive oil and parsley to the soup, taste and adjust the seasoning if necessary.

5 Toast the bread and put a slice in the base of 4 warmed soup bowls. Ladle the soup over the bread and serve immediately.

*cook's tip

Italian cooks would probably slice off the cheeks from the fish head and add them to the soup.

Overleaf *Sienna is situated in the center of Tuscany. It is famous for its history and Gothic architecture*

marinated raw beef
carpaccio

SERVES 4

7 oz. fillet of beef, in 1 piece

2 tbsp. lemon juice

salt and pepper

4 tbsp. extra virgin olive oil

2 oz. Parmesan cheese, shaved thinly

4 tbsp. chopped fresh flat-leaf parsley

lemon slices, to garnish

ciabatta or focaccia, to serve

1 Using a very sharp knife, cut the beef fillet into wafer-thin slices and arrange on 4 individual serving plates.

2 Pour the lemon juice into a small bowl and season to taste with salt and pepper. Whisk in the olive oil, then pour the dressing over the meat. Cover the plates with plastic wrap and set aside for 10–15 minutes to marinate.

3 Remove and discard the plastic wrap. Arrange the Parmesan shavings in the center of each serving and sprinkle with parsley. Garnish with lemon slices and serve with fresh bread.

variation

To make *carpaccio di tonno*, substitute fresh, uncooked tuna for the fillet of beef. Do not use thawed frozen fish, and eat on the day of purchase.

You need extremely thin slices of meat for this recipe. If you place the beef in the freezer for about 30 minutes, you will find it easier to slice.

prosciutto with arugula

prosciutto con la rucola

Arugula has become a fashionable salad vegetable in many homes and restaurants, but it has never been out of favor in Italy, where it grows wild.

SERVES 4

4 oz. arugula

1 tbsp. lemon juice

salt and pepper

3 tbsp. extra virgin olive oil

8 oz. prosciutto, sliced thinly

1 Separate the arugula leaves, wash in cold water, and pat dry on paper towels. Place the leaves in a bowl.

2 Pour the lemon juice into a small bowl and season to taste with salt and pepper. Whisk in the olive oil, then pour the dressing over the arugula leaves and toss lightly so they are evenly coated.

3 Carefully drape the prosciutto in folds on 4 individual serving plates, then add the arugula. Serve at room temperature.

variation

For a more substantial salad, add 1 thinly sliced fennel bulb and 2 thinly sliced oranges to the arugula in step 1. Substitute orange juice or balsamic vinegar for the lemon juice in step 2.

48 mixed antipasto meat platter
salumi

The town of San Daniele competes with Parma for the prize for the best cured ham (prosciutto), while Milan stakes its claim for the tastiest salami against stiff competition from Naples, Rome, and Cremona. Let your taste buds be the judges.

SERVES 4

1 cantaloupe

2 oz. Italian salami, sliced thinly

8 slices prosciutto

8 slices bresaola

8 slices mortadella

4 plum tomatoes, sliced thinly

4 fresh figs, quartered

⅔ cup black olive,* pitted

2 tbsp. shredded fresh basil leaves

4 tbsp. extra virgin olive oil, plus extra for serving

pepper

1 Cut the melon in half, scoop out and discard the seeds, then cut the flesh into 8 wedges. Arrange the wedges on one half of a large serving platter.

2 Arrange the salami, prosciutto, bresaola, and mortadella in loose folds on the other half of the platter. Arrange the tomato slices and fig quarters along the center of the platter.

3 Sprinkle the olives over the meat. Sprinkle the basil over the tomatoes and drizzle with olive oil. Season to taste with pepper, then serve with extra olive oil.

*cook's tip

For extra flavor, make up your own marinated olives. Combine 2⅔ cups pitted black olives, 1 sliced garlic clove, 1 red chili, 3 slices lemon, and 2 tablespoons red wine vinegar and mix well. Transfer to a screw-top jar and add enough extra virgin olive oil to cover. Screw on the lid and leave at room temperature for 2 weeks.

The Pantheon in Rome was built as a temple to the gods 2,000 years ago. It has a famous round opening, or oculus, in its roof

polenta with prosciutto
polenta con prosciutto

These tasty morsels are ideal appetizers when you are entertaining, because they can be prepared in advance and then popped under the broiler when you are ready to serve.

SERVES 6

2¹/₂ **cups water**

⁵/₈ **cup quick-cook cornmeal**

¹/₄ **cup freshly grated Parmesan cheese**

2 **tbsp. butter, softened**

salt and pepper

extra virgin olive oil, to serve

for the topping

2 **tbsp. extra virgin olive oil, plus extra for greasing**

6 **slices prosciutto crudo**

3 **oz. fontina cheese, cut into 6 slices**

12 **fresh sage leaves**

1 Line a 6 x 10-inch jelly roll pan with parchment paper and set aside.

2 Pour the measured water into a large pan and bring to a boil. Reduce the heat so that it is just simmering and add a large pinch of salt. Add the cornmeal in a steady stream, stirring constantly. Let simmer, stirring, for 5 minutes, until thickened.

3 Remove the pan from the heat and stir in the Parmesan and butter and season to taste with pepper. Spoon the polenta evenly into the pan and smooth the surface with a spatula. Set aside to cool completely.

4 Oil a baking sheet and a 3-inch plain, round cookie cutter. Turn out the polenta, stamp out 6 circles, and place on the baking sheet. Brush with olive oil and season with salt and pepper.

5 Cook under a preheated broiler for 3–4 minutes. Turn the circles over, brush with more oil, and broil for an additional 3–4 minutes, until golden. Remove from the broiler and, if you are not serving immediately, set the circles aside to cool completely.

6 Drape a slice of ham on each polenta circle and top with a slice of fontina. Brush the sage leaves with some of the remaining olive oil and place 2 on each polenta circle.

7 Cook the polenta circles under a preheated broiler for 3–4 minutes, until the cheese has melted and the sage is crisp. Serve immediately with extra olive oil for dipping.

variation

Substitute crumbled Gorgonzola cheese for the grated Parmesan.

52 roman artichokes
carciofi alla romana

The Roman contribution to this dish of stuffed artichokes is to flavor it with mint. Italian or Roman mint has a particularly sweet flavor, but you could use ordinary garden mint or one of the more exciting varieties, such as lemon or apple mint.

SERVES 4

5 tbsp. lemon juice

4 globe artichokes

1 garlic clove

4 sprigs fresh flat-leaf parsley

2 sprigs fresh mint

1 lemon, quartered

4 tbsp. olive oil

salt and pepper

2 tbsp. dry, uncolored bread crumbs

2 garlic cloves, chopped finely

2 tbsp. fresh flat-leaf parsley,
chopped coarsely

2 tbsp. fresh mint, chopped coarsely

1 tbsp. unsalted butter, diced

1 Select a bowl large enough to accommodate the prepared artichokes and fill with cold water and 4 tablespoons of the lemon juice. Working on one artichoke at a time, snap off the stems, then peel away the tough outer leaves. Snip or break off the tough tops of the remaining leaves. When the central cone of the artichoke appears, cut off the top ¾ inch with a sharp knife. Drop the prepared artichokes into the acidulated water to prevent them from discoloring.

2 Place the artichokes in a heavy-bottom pan that is large enough to hold them firmly upright in a single layer. Add the whole garlic clove, parsley sprigs, mint sprigs, lemon quarters, and olive oil, and season to taste with salt and pepper. Pour in enough water to come two-thirds of the way up the sides. Bring to a boil over low heat, cover tightly, and let simmer for about 15 minutes, until nearly tender.

3 Meanwhile, combine the bread crumbs, chopped garlic, parsley, and mint in a bowl, and season to taste with salt and pepper.

4 Remove the artichokes from the pan and set aside to cool slightly. When they are cold enough to handle, gently separate the leaves, remove the central bearded chokes or cones with a teaspoon and discard. Season the artichokes to taste with salt and pepper. Return them to the pan, again standing them upright in a single layer. Spoon the bread crumb mixture into the centers, cover tightly, and cook over low heat for 20–30 minutes, until tender.

5 Using a slotted spoon, transfer the artichokes to 4 individual serving plates and set aside. Strain the cooking liquid into a clean pan and bring to a boil over high heat. Cook until reduced by about one-quarter or until the juices are concentrated, then reduce the heat and stir in the remaining lemon juice. Add the butter, a piece at a time, swirling the sauce in the pan until the butter has melted. Do not let the sauce boil. When all the butter has been incorporated, remove the pan from the heat. Serve the artichokes still warm and pass around the sauce separately.

54 warm vegetable medley
caponata

This melt-in-the-mouth mixture of tomatoes, eggplants, and celery, flavored with garlic and capers, is a traditional Sicilian appetizer.

SERVES 4

4 tbsp. olive oil

2 celery stalks, sliced

2 red onions, sliced

1 lb. eggplant, diced

1 garlic clove, chopped finely

5 plum tomatoes, chopped

3 tbsp. red wine vinegar

1 tbsp. sugar

3 tbsp. green olives, pitted

2 tbsp. capers*

salt and pepper

4 tbsp. chopped fresh flat-leaf parsley

ciabatta or panini, to serve

1 Heat half the olive oil in a large, heavy-bottom pan. Add the celery and onions and cook over low heat, stirring occasionally, for 5 minutes, until softened but not colored. Add the remaining oil and the eggplant. Cook, stirring frequently, for about 5 minutes, until the eggplant starts to color.

2 Add the garlic, tomatoes, vinegar, and sugar, and mix well. Cover the mixture with a circle of waxed paper and let simmer gently for about 10 minutes.

3 Remove the waxed paper, stir in the olives and capers, and season to taste with salt and pepper. Pour the caponata into a serving dish and set aside to cool to room temperature. Sprinkle the parsley over the vegetables and serve with fresh bread or rolls.

*cook's tip

If possible, buy Sicilian capers for this dish. They are simply packed in salt and just need rinsing before use. Otherwise, use capers pickled in brine, but avoid those that are bottled in vinegar.

cheese and sun-dried tomato toasts

bruschetta

These tempting morsels make delicious canapés to serve with drinks or as an excellent appetizer.

SERVES 4

2 sfilatini*

³/₄ cup sun-dried tomato paste

10¹/₂ oz. mozzarella di bufala, drained and diced

1¹/₂ tsp. dried oregano

2–3 tbsp. olive oil

pepper

***cook's tip**

If you are unable to find sfilatini, use a large ciabatta and cut the slices in half.

1 Slice the loaves diagonally and discard the end pieces. Toast the slices on both sides under a preheated broiler until golden.

2 Spread one side of each toast with the sun-dried tomato paste and top with mozzarella. Sprinkle with oregano and season to taste with pepper.

3 Place the toasts on a large baking sheet and drizzle with olive oil. Bake in a preheated oven, 425°F, for about 5 minutes, until the cheese has melted and is bubbling. Remove the hot toasts from the oven and let them stand for 5 minutes before serving.

56

sicilian stuffed tomatoes
pomodori alla siciliana

1 Cut a thin slice off the tops of the tomatoes and discard. Scoop out the seeds with a teaspoon and discard, taking care not to pierce the shells. Turn the tomato shells upside down on paper towels to drain.

2 Heat 6 tablespoons of the olive oil in a skillet, add the onions and garlic, and cook over low heat, stirring occasionally, for 5 minutes, until softened. Remove the skillet from the heat and stir in the bread crumbs, anchovies, olives, and herbs.

3 Using a teaspoon, fill the tomato shells with the bread crumb mixture, then place in an ovenproof dish large enough to hold them in a single layer. Sprinkle the tops with grated Parmesan and drizzle with the remaining oil.

4 Bake in a preheated oven, 350°F, for 20–25 minutes, until the tomatoes are tender and the topping is golden brown.

5 Remove the dish from the oven and serve immediately, if serving hot, or let cool to room temperature.

A classic combination of sun-ripened tomatoes, black olives, anchovies, and fresh herbs, this recipe is simplicity itself. It is best eaten, Italian-style, at room temperature, but you can serve it hot, if you prefer.

SERVES 4

8 large, ripe tomatoes

7 tbsp. extra virgin olive oil

2 onions, finely chopped

2 garlic cloves, crushed

2 cups fresh bread crumbs

8 anchovy fillets in oil, drained and chopped

3 tbsp. black olives, pitted and chopped

2 tbsp. chopped fresh flat-leaf parsley

1 tbsp. chopped fresh oregano

4 tbsp. freshly grated Parmesan cheese

Italy's Amalfi coast is made up of small fishing villages, such as Minori, that are situated on steep cliffs

58 fried cheese sandwiches
mozzarella in carrozza

This Neapolitan speciality is one of the nicest ways to serve mozzarella cheese. It makes a wonderful snack for two people, as well as a superb appetizer for four.

SERVES 4

for the sauce

3 tbsp. olive oil

1 onion, chopped

2 garlic cloves, chopped finely

1 red bell pepper, seeded and chopped

14 oz. canned tomatoes, chopped

2 tbsp. tomato paste

1 tbsp. lemon juice

2 tbsp. water

salt and pepper

7 oz. mozzarella di bufala

8 1/2-in. thick slices day-old white bread, crusts removed

3 oz. unsalted butter

4 medium slices Italian salami

corn oil, for deep-frying

3 eggs

3 tbsp. milk

salt and pepper

1 First, make the sauce. Heat the olive oil in a medium, heavy-bottom pan. Add the onion and garlic and cook over low heat, stirring occasionally, for 5 minutes, until softened. Add the red bell pepper and cook, stirring frequently, for an additional 5 minutes. Stir in the tomatoes, tomato paste, lemon juice, and water, and season to taste with salt and pepper. Cover the pan and let simmer for about 15 minutes, until pulpy.

2 Meanwhile, slice the mozzarella into 4 thick or 8 medium slices. Spread the bread slices with the butter and place the mozzarella on 4 of them. Top with the salami and sandwich together with the remaining slices of bread. Cut in half to make triangles, wrap in plastic wrap, and let chill in the refrigerator.

3 Remove the sauce from the heat and set aside to cool slightly in the pan, then process in a food processor or blender until smooth. Return the sauce to a clean pan and reheat gently.

4 Heat the corn oil in a deep-fryer to 350–375°F or, if using a heavy-bottom pan, until a cube of day-old bread browns in 30 seconds. Meanwhile, beat the eggs with the milk in a shallow dish and season to taste with salt and pepper. Unwrap the sandwiches and dip them, in batches, into the egg mixture, letting them soak briefly. Add the sandwiches, in batches, to the hot oil and cook until golden brown on both sides. Remove with tongs, drain well on paper towels, and keep warm while you cook the remaining triangles. Serve the sandwiches hot and pass around the sauce separately.

PASTA, RICE, & PIZZA

62 Ask a room full of people to name an Italian dish and the chances are some would say pasta, others risotto, and still others pizza. If you then asked the pasta lovers for a specific recipe, they would probably all name a different one—and so would aficionados of rice and pizza. In other words, these three are well-loved staples, not only in Italy but throughout the world.

pasta

For many people, pasta is Italian cooking and most certainly it is served frequently and in almost every part of the country. Traditionally, it forms the first of two lunchtime courses, rather than being a main dish as is often the case outside Italy. As well as being inexpensive, filling, and nourishing, pasta is immensely versatile and goes well with a vast range of ingredients—vegetables, mushrooms, meat, fish, seafood, herbs, and cheese—or a simple drizzle of the best extra virgin olive oil. Sauces may be simple or elaborate, time-consuming or quick and easy, but, as with all Italian cooking, their success depends on using the best-quality and freshest ingredients.

The recipes each suggest a suitable pasta variety, but there is no reason why you shouldn't substitute your own favorites. For example, Bolognese Sauce (see page 70) is traditionally served with tagliatelle, but spaghetti is already a popular alternative and other ribbon pastas would work equally well. You could substitute a flavored pasta for a plain one to create a more colorful dish or use a mixture for an attractive *tricolore* effect.

Baked pasta dishes, such as the classic *lasagne al forno* (see page 79), are heart-warming on a chilly

Success depends on using the best-quality and freshest ingredients

winter's day, and simpler and lighter recipes, such as *farfalle all'alfredo* (see page 74) would be the perfect *primo* for an alfresco lunch. If speed is of the essence, what could be simpler than *linguine alla puttanesca* (see page 90)?

Fresh pasta is typical of northern Italy, and dried pasta is more usual in the south, but it is really a matter of personal taste which you prefer to use.

What is important is that it is cooked until it is just tender. It is a mistake to drain it too thoroughly, and once cooked, it should be tossed immediately with the sauce or with a little butter or olive oil to prevent it from drying out.

The Colosseum in Rome is the most visited monument in Italy

64

how to cook pasta

There is a right way to cook pasta so that it is *al dente*—tender but still firm to the bite. Bring a large pan of lightly salted water to a boil. Add the pasta and bring the water back to a boil. Start timing as soon the water returns to a boil. Do not simmer pasta or it will become sticky—the water should be boiling fast, uncovered. Fresh pasta takes only a few minutes, while most dried pasta requires 8–10 minutes. However, cooking times can vary (check the package instructions), and you should start testing about 2 minutes before you think it will be ready. The easiest way to test is to remove a small piece and bite it between your front teeth. If it is tender, but not soggy, the pasta is cooked. Drain it right away and quickly in a colander. It is better if the pasta is not thoroughly drained. Immediately toss with the prepared sauce or with olive oil. Do not leave pasta standing before serving or it will become sticky and unappetizing. Some cooks add a tablespoon of olive oil to the cooking water to prevent the pasta from sticking. This is not necessary if there is plenty of water and it is boiling vigorously.

which pasta?

There are no fixed rules about which sauce partners with which pasta shape, but there are traditional recipes and also a few helpful guidelines. Sauces that cling, such as those made with eggs, cream, grated cheese, olive oil, butter, and herbs, are ideal with long thin pasta. Chunky sauces go well with pasta shapes that can hold them like tiny cups.

Plain dried pasta is off-white, and egg pasta has a more golden color. Pasta may also be colored and flavored by adding other ingredients to the dough. Spinach (green) and tomato (red) are very common and, combined with plain pasta, make *pasta tricolore*. Green and yellow egg pasta ribbons are known as *paglia e fieno*—straw and hay. Squid or cuttlefish ink

produces dramatic-looking black pasta that contrasts superbly with shellfish for a dinner party, and beet produces a deep magenta color. Other flavorings and colorings include porcini and other mushrooms, chilies and bell peppers. Whole-wheat pasta in a limited number of shapes is also available.

long pasta

Bavette: narrow, oval pasta, popular in the south.
Bucatini: hollow pasta, slightly thicker than spaghetti. Popular in Sicily and Rome.
Capelli d'angelo: "angel hair" pasta that is very fine and usually sold in nests. Typically used in soups or for serving to children.
Chitarra: "guitar" pasta, so named after the wire-strung wooden frames on which it is cut. It has a square cross-section.
Fettuccelle: straight, flat pasta ribbons.

Fettuccine: flat, quite narrow pasta ribbons, originally from Rome and still common in Lazio. Fettuccine are sold in nests.

Fusilli lunghi: long pasta like an extended corkscrew.

Lasagnette: wide, flat pasta. Lasagnette sometimes have wavy edges.

Linguine: "little tongues." Thin, spaghetti-like pasta.

Linguinette: very thin, spaghetti-like pasta.

Maccheroni: refers to long, thick, hollow pasta tubes in northern Italy, whereas in the south, the term usually refers to small pasta. Maccheroni is also used as a generic term for any pasta.

Nastroni: short, wide pasta ribbons, like shavings.

Pappardelle: wide pasta ribbons, which may have one wavy edge. Usually made from egg pasta.

Spaghetti: "little strings." Thin, hollow pasta tubes.

Spaghettini: very thin, hollow pasta tubes.

Tagliarini: flat pasta ribbons, thinner than tagliatelle.

Tagliatelle: flat pasta ribbons, originally from Bologna. Sold in nests.

Tonnarelli: flat pasta ribbons, similar to tagliatelle. Sold in nests.

Trenette: narrow ribbons, usually made from egg pasta and originally from the Liguria region, where they are traditionally served with the classic basil sauce, pesto.

Vermicelli: "little worms." Very fine, hollow pasta.

Zite: "fiancées," so called because they were traditionally served at wedding celebrations in southern Italy. Long, thick, hollow tubes.

short pasta

There are hundreds of different shapes and even more names because the same shape may be called something different in another region. New shapes are being developed all the time.

Benfatti: "well made," ironically so called because it consists of scraps and offcuts of pasta from making other shapes.

Chifferi: small, curved tubes, which may be ridged. Also called *chifferini, chifferoni,* and *chifferotti.*

Conchiglie: shell-shaped pasta that is extremely popular because it traps sauces inside. Varies in size from tiny soup pasta to large shells that can be filled. *Conchiglie rigate* are ridged.

Eliche: "propeller," so called because of their spiral shape. Eliche are easily confused with fusilli. Available in a range of sizes and colors.

Elicoidali: "helixes." Short, narrow, hollow pasta tubes, with curved ridges.

Farfalle: "butterflies," this bow-shaped pasta is available in a range of colors and may be ridged.

Fusilli: "rifles," so named because they are spirals that closely resemble the barrel of a gun in shape. They can be distinguished from eliche by the fact the spiral opens out, rather than remaining firm. Unlike eliche, fusilli are rarely colored.

Garganelli: tubular egg pasta that has been rolled like a scroll. A speciality of Emilia-Romagna.

Gemelli: "twins." So called because two strips of pasta are twisted together.

Lumache: "snails," shell-shaped pasta, that may be ridged (*lumache rigate*).

Maccheroni: small, hollow, bent pasta tubes. This usage is particularly common in southern Italy, whereas in the north, maccheroni usually refers to long pasta. The word is also used as a generic term for any pasta.

Orecchiette: "little ears." Small, flat pasta shapes that are a speciality of Puglia. They have a chewy texture.

Penne: "quills," so called because the hollow pasta tubes have diagonally cut ends, like a quill pen. They may be smooth (*penne lisce*) or ridged (*penne rigate*). Very popular both inside and outside Italy.

Pipe: "pipes." Small, hollow, bent pasta tubes. Most often available as *pipe rigate*, ridged tubes.

Radiatori: "radiators." Pasta shaped like an old-fashioned radiator! Good for holding sauce.

Rigatoni: chunky, hollow, ridged shapes.

Rotelle or Ruote: "wheels," so called because they resemble cart wheels. Very popular with children and available in different colors. They are also known as *ruote di carro*.

Strozzapreti: "priest stranglers," so called because they consist of two strands of pasta twisted together. The polite version of the story is that they got their name from a priest who liked them so much, he gobbled his food and choked. The more likely explanation lies in the historic hostility between church and state.

soup pasta

There are hundreds of tiny pasta shapes, called pastina, for adding to clear soups and broths.

Acini di pepe: "peppercorns."

Alfabeti: medium-size, alphabet shapes, which are very popular with children.

Anellini: "rings." Small to medium hoops. Anellini are sometimes ridged.

Conchigliette: "small shells."

Farfalline: "small butterflies."

Fregola: tiny shapes resembling couscous. A speciality of Sardinia.

Funghetti: "small mushrooms."

Lumachine: "small snails."

Occhi: tiny pasta shapes.

Orecchiettini: "tiny ears."

Orzi: "barley."

Risi: "rice."

Semi di melone: "melon seeds."

Stelle: "stars." Medium-size soup pasta.

Stellette: "small stars."

Tubetti: "small tubes."

pasta for baking

Pasta layered with meat, fish, or vegetable sauce, coated in a creamy béchamel and sprinkled with cheese before baking in the oven is invariably made with lasagna or a variation of it. It can also be filled and rolled up before baking, rather like cannelloni.

Lasagna: dry pasta sheets that may be rectangular or square and plain, green, or whole-wheat. Some versions have curly edges. Traditional lasagna requires precooking before layering it in the dish. To precook: plunge 3 or 4 sheets into a large pan of lightly salted water and boil for about 8 minutes (check the package instructions) until tender, but still firm to the bite. Remove with tongs and lay the sheets flat on a clean, damp dish towel, while you cook the remaining sheets. No-precook pasta can be layered straight from the package into the dish, but may take longer to cook.

filled pasta

Agnolotti: half-moon shaped filled pasta, with a crinkled edge. A speciality of the Piedmont, they are traditionally filled with meat.

Cannelloni: "large reeds." Pasta tubes, which may be plain, spinach, or whole-wheat. Use a teaspoon or pastry bag to fill them. They are larger than ravioli or tortellini, so various fillings are possible.

Cappelletti: "little hats." Pasta squares are folded diagonally around a filling, then two of the ends are wrapped around an edge to make a brim. A speciality of Emilia-Romagna, they are traditionally filled with ground meat and cheese. They are served in clear broth at Christmas.

Pansotti: pasta squares are filled, then folded into triangles, with a bulge in the center. A speciality of Liguria, they are traditionally filled with pecorino cheese, hard-cooked eggs, and spinach, and served with a walnut sauce.

Ravioli: all-purpose filled pasta, which are usually square but may also be rectangular, round, or oval. The edges are fluted. Ravioli are sometimes served in a clear broth.

Tortellini: pasta dough rounds are folded, then wrapped around a finger and the ends tucked in to resemble Venus's navel, apparently. A speciality of Bologna, they are traditionally filled with ground meat and prosciutto. Tortellini are served in a clear broth at Christmas.

Tortelloni: a larger version of tortellini.

rice

Rice is accorded much greater standing in Italy than it is in many other countries. It is never served plain or regarded as a mere accompaniment to more exciting ingredients. Risotto—meaning little rice—forms a course on its own, which is considered just as important as the meat or fish that is to follow. The dish was created to exploit the particular characteristics of Italian rice varieties and it is essential to use risotto rice to achieve the unique creamy texture. It is typical of Italian cooking that time and care are lavished on its preparation—you

Sauces that cling such as those made with eggs, cream, grated cheese, olive oil, butter, and herbs, are ideal with long thin pasta

cannot hurry a risotto. The liquid should always be added a ladleful at a time and the risotto stirred constantly until it has all been absorbed.

Risottos may be based on a wide variety of ingredients—vegetables, seafood, mushrooms, chicken, or cheese—but they are never made from leftovers. Some, such as *risotto ai quattro formaggi* (see page 99), are wonderfully rich, whereas others, such as *risotto alla Milanese* (see page 98), are deceptively simple. All are attractive and appetizing.

pizza

There can be few places in the world where the word "pizza" is unknown, and these days you will find pizzas with toppings that range from the basic to the bizarre. Traditional pizzas, however, rarely have a huge mass of ingredients that fight for the attention of our taste buds. In characteristic Italian style, a few harmonious and well-balanced flavors are preferred.

The classic cheese for pizza is mozzarella because of its superb melting qualities. It is no coincidence that the best mozzarella comes from the area around Naples, the city that invented the pizza. It is worth buying good-quality mozzarella, preferably one made from buffalo's milk. Try to avoid the semihard, yellow mozzarella, sometimes ready-grated and sold specifically for pizzas.

Overleaf Numerous buildings in cities such as Venice have traditional façades that date back many centuries

70 tagliatelle with a rich meat sauce
tagliatelle alla bolognese

One of the world's best-known and most-loved pasta dishes, Bologna's meat sauce—ragù—is classically served not with spaghetti but with tagliatelle. Do use steak, not ordinary ground beef.

SERVES 4

4 tbsp. olive oil, plus extra for serving

3 oz. pancetta or rindless lean bacon, diced

1 onion, chopped

1 garlic clove, chopped finely

1 carrot, chopped

1 celery stalk, chopped

1 cup ground steak

4 oz. chicken livers, chopped

2 tbsp. strained tomatoes

1/2 cup dry white wine

1 cup beef stock or water

1 tbsp. chopped fresh oregano

1 bay leaf

salt and pepper

1 lb. dried tagliatelle

freshly grated Parmesan cheese, to serve

1 Heat the olive oil in a large, heavy-bottom pan. Add the pancetta or bacon and cook over medium heat, stirring occasionally, for 3–5 minutes, until it is just turning brown. Add the onion, garlic, carrot, and celery and cook, stirring occasionally, for an additional 5 minutes.

2 Add the steak and cook over high heat, breaking up the meat with a wooden spoon, for 5 minutes, until browned. Stir in the chicken livers and cook, stirring occasionally, for an additional 2–3 minutes. Add the strained tomatoes, wine, stock, oregano, and bay leaf, and season to taste with salt and pepper. Bring to a boil, reduce the heat, cover, and simmer for 30–35 minutes.*

3 When the sauce is almost cooked, bring a large pan of lightly salted water to a boil. Add the pasta, bring back to a boil, and cook for 8–10 minutes, until tender but still firm to the bite. Drain, transfer to a warmed serving dish, drizzle with a little olive oil, and toss well.

4 Remove and discard the bay leaf from the sauce, then pour it over the pasta, toss again, and serve immediately with grated Parmesan.

*cook's tip
You can also layer this sauce with sheets of lasagna and Béchamel Sauce (see page 79) and bake the dish in the oven.

Pasta, rice, and pizza form the basis of a menu at an Italian restaurant and the cuisine has spread worldwide

spaghetti with meatballs
spaghetti con le polpette

Every Italian "mama" has her own version of this dish, which, naturally, is the very best.

SERVES 6

1 potato, diced

1³/₄ cups ground steak

1 onion, finely chopped

1 egg

4 tbsp. chopped fresh flat-leaf parsley

all-purpose flour, for dusting

5 tbsp. virgin olive oil

1³/₄ cups strained tomatoes

2 tbsp. tomato paste

14 oz. dried spaghetti

salt and pepper

for the garnish

6 fresh basil leaves, shredded

freshly grated Parmesan cheese

1 Place the potato in a small pan, add cold water to cover and a pinch of salt, and bring to a boil. Cook for 10–15 minutes, until tender, then drain. Either mash thoroughly with a potato masher or fork or pass through a potato ricer.

2 Combine the potato, steak, onion, egg, and parsley in a bowl and season to taste with salt and pepper. Spread out the flour on a plate. With dampened hands, shape the meat mixture into walnut-size balls and roll in the flour. Shake off any excess.

3 Heat the oil in a heavy-bottom skillet, add the meatballs, and cook over medium heat, stirring and turning frequently, for 8–10 minutes, until golden all over.

4 Add the strained tomatoes and tomato paste and cook for an additional 10 minutes, until the sauce is reduced and thickened.

5 Meanwhile, bring a large pan of lightly salted water to a boil. Add the pasta, bring back to a boil, and cook for 8–10 minutes, until tender but still firm to the bite.

6 Drain well and add to the meatball sauce, tossing well to coat. Transfer to a warmed serving dish, garnish with the basil leaves and Parmesan, and serve immediately.

74

farfalle with cream and parmesan
farfalle all'alfredo

SERVES 4

1 lb. dried farfalle

1 oz. unsalted butter

²/₃ cup heavy cream

pinch of freshly grated nutmeg

salt and pepper

to finish

4 tbsp. heavy cream

¹/₂ cup freshly grated Parmesan cheese,
  plus extra to serve

This classic Roman dish is simplicity itself, but tastes just wonderful.

1 Bring a large pan of lightly salted water to a boil. Add the pasta, bring back to a boil, and cook for 8–10 minutes, until tender but still firm to the bite, then drain thoroughly.

2 Put the butter and cream in a large, heavy-bottom pan and bring to a boil. Reduce the heat and let simmer for 1 minute, until slightly thickened.

3 Add the drained pasta to the cream mixture. Place the pan over low heat and toss until the farfalle are thoroughly coated. Season to taste with nutmeg, salt, and pepper, then add the cream and grated Parmesan. Toss again and serve immediately with extra Parmesan for sprinkling.

variation

For a more substantial dish, melt the butter on its own in step 2 and add generous 2 cups petits pois. Cook for 2–3 minutes, add the cream, and continue as above.

fusilli with gorgonzola and mushroom sauce
fusilli alla boscaiola

This aromatic pasta sauce sums up the Italian approach to cooking—a few, fairly basic ingredients, but they must be of the best quality possible.

SERVES 4

12 oz. dried fusilli

3 tbsp. olive oil

12 oz. exotic mushrooms,* sliced

1 garlic clove, chopped finely

1³/₄ cups heavy cream

9 oz. Gorgonzola cheese, crumbled

salt and pepper

2 tbsp. chopped fresh flat–leaf parsley, to garnish

1 Bring a large pan of lightly salted water to a boil. Add the pasta, bring back to a boil, and cook for 8–10 minutes, until tender but still firm to the bite.

2 Meanwhile, heat the olive oil in a heavy-bottom pan. Add the mushrooms and cook over low heat, stirring frequently, for 5 minutes. Add the garlic and cook for an additional 2 minutes.

3 Add the cream, bring to a boil, and cook for 1 minute, until slightly thickened. Stir in the cheese and cook over low heat until it has melted. Do not let the sauce boil once the cheese has been added. Season to taste with salt and pepper and remove the pan from the heat.

4 Drain the pasta and pour it into the sauce. Toss well to coat, then serve immediately, garnished with the parsley.

*cook's tip

Exotic mushrooms have a much earthier flavor than cultivated ones, so they complement the strong taste of the cheese. Porcini are especially delicious but rather expensive. Portobello mushrooms, if you can find them, would also be a good choice. Otherwise, use cultivated mushrooms, but add ¼ cup dried porcini, soaked for 20 minutes in 1 cup hot water and then drained.

76 baked pasta with mushrooms
crostata ai funghi

A crostata may be a tart or, as in this case, a casserole of pasta, béchamel sauce, and a tasty filling.

SERVES 4

5 oz. fontina cheese, sliced thinly

1 quantity hot Béchamel Sauce (see page 79)

3 oz. butter, plus extra for greasing

12 oz. mixed exotic mushrooms, sliced

12 oz. dried tagliatelle

2 egg yolks

salt and pepper

4 tbsp. freshly grated pecorino cheese

1 Stir the fontina cheese into the béchamel sauce and set aside.

2 Melt 1 oz. of the butter in a large pan. Add the mushrooms and cook over low heat, stirring occasionally, for 10 minutes.

3 Meanwhile, bring a large pan of lightly salted water to a boil. Add the pasta, bring back to a boil, and cook for 8–10 minutes, until tender but still firm to the bite. Drain, return to the pan, and add the remaining butter, the egg yolks, and about one-third of the sauce, then season to taste with salt and pepper. Toss well to mix, then gently stir in the mushrooms.

4 Lightly grease a large, ovenproof dish and spoon in the pasta mixture. Pour over the remaining sauce evenly and sprinkle with the grated pecorino.

5 Bake in a preheated oven, 400°F, for 15–20 minutes, until golden brown. Serve immediately.

The Duomo, or cathedral, in Florence

baked lasagna
lasagne al forno

1 First, make the meat sauce. Heat the olive oil in a large, heavy-bottom pan. Add the onion, celery, carrot, pancetta, beef, and pork, and cook over medium heat, stirring frequently and breaking up the meat with a wooden spoon, for 10 minutes, until lightly browned.

2 Add the wine, bring to a boil, and cook until reduced. Add about two-thirds of the stock, bring to a boil, and cook until reduced. Combine the remaining stock and tomato paste and add to the pan. Season to taste, add the clove, the bay leaf, and pour in the milk. Cover and let simmer over low heat for 1½ hours.

3 Next, make the béchamel sauce. Melt the butter, add the flour, and cook over low heat, stirring constantly, for 1 minute. Remove the pan from the heat and gradually stir in the milk. Return the pan to the heat and bring to a boil, stirring constantly, until thickened and smooth. Add the bay leaf and let simmer gently for 2 minutes. Remove the bay leaf and season the sauce to taste with salt, pepper, and nutmeg. Remove the pan from the heat and set aside.

4 Unless you are using lasagna that needs no precooking, bring a large pan of lightly salted water to a boil. Add the lasagna sheets, in batches, bring back to a boil, and cook for about 10 minutes, until tender but still firm to the bite. Remove with tongs and spread out on a clean dish towel.

5 Remove the meat sauce from the heat and discard the clove and bay leaf. Lightly grease a large, oven-proof dish with butter. Place a layer of the pasta in the base and cover it with a layer of meat sauce. Spoon a layer of béchamel sauce on top and sprinkle with one-third of the mozzarella and Parmesan cheeses. Continue making layers until all the ingredients are used, ending with a topping of béchamel sauce and sprinkled cheese.

6 Dot the top of the lasagna with the diced butter and bake in a preheated oven, 400°F, for 30 minutes, until golden and bubbling.

You need plenty of time to make a baked lasagna with an authentic flavor, but it is worth it.

SERVES 4

for the meat sauce

3 tbsp. olive oil

1 onion, chopped finely

1 celery stick, chopped finely

1 carrot, chopped finely

3½ oz. pancetta or rindless lean bacon, chopped finely

¾ cup ground beef

¾ cup ground pork

scant ½ cup dry red wine

⅔ cup beef stock

1 tbsp. tomato paste

salt and pepper

1 clove

1 bay leaf

⅔ cup boiling milk

for the Béchamel Sauce

2 oz. unsalted butter

⅜ cup all-purpose flour

generous 2 cups milk

1 bay leaf

salt and pepper

pinch of freshly grated nutmeg

14 oz. dried lasagna verdi

5 oz. mozzarella cheese, drained and diced

1¼ cups freshly grated Parmesan cheese

2 oz. unsalted butter, diced, plus extra for greasing

80

cannelloni with spinach and ricotta
cannelloni imbottiti

Creamy ricotta cheese and spinach is a favorite Italian combination that appears in many guises. This pasta dish originated in the Emilia-Romagna region.

SERVES 4

12 dried cannelloni tubes, 3-in. long

butter, for greasing

for the filling

5 oz. lean ham,* chopped

³/₄ cup frozen spinach, thawed and drained

scant ¹/₂ cup ricotta cheese

1 egg

3 tbsp. freshly grated pecorino cheese

pinch of freshly grated nutmeg

salt and pepper

for the cheese sauce

2¹/₂ cups milk

1 oz. unsalted butter

2 tbsp. all-purpose flour

³/₄ cup freshly grated Gruyère cheese

salt and pepper

1 Bring a large pan of lightly salted water to a boil. Add the cannelloni tubes, bring back to a boil, and cook for 6–7 minutes, until nearly tender. Drain and rinse under cold water. Spread out the tubes on a clean dish towel.

2 Put the ham, spinach, and ricotta into a food processor and process for a few seconds until combined. Add the egg and pecorino and process again to a smooth paste. Scrape the filling into a bowl and season to taste with nutmeg, salt, and pepper.

3 Grease an ovenproof dish with butter. Spoon the filling into a pastry bag fitted with a ¹/₂-inch nozzle. Carefully open one cannelloni tube, stand it upright, and pipe in the filling. Place the filled tube in the dish and continue to fill the remaining cannelloni.

4 To make the cheese sauce, heat the milk to just below boiling point. Meanwhile, melt the butter in another pan. Add the flour to the butter and cook over low heat, stirring constantly, for 1 minute. Remove the pan from the heat and gradually stir in the hot milk. Return the pan to the heat and bring to a boil, stirring constantly. Let simmer over the lowest possible heat, stirring frequently, for 10 minutes, until thickened and smooth. Remove the pan from the heat, stir in the Gruyère, and season to taste with salt and pepper.

5 Spoon the cheese sauce over the filled cannelloni. Cover the dish with foil and bake in a preheated oven, 350°F, for 20–25 minutes. Serve immediately.

*cook's tip

For a vegetarian version of this dish, simply omit the ham or substitute the same weight of mushrooms.

springtime pasta
pasta primavera

Globe artichokes grow wild in Sicily and are cultivated throughout Italy, but they are always considered a speciality of Roman cooking.

SERVES 4

2 tbsp. lemon juice

4 baby globe artichokes

7 tbsp. olive oil

2 shallots, chopped finely

2 garlic cloves, chopped finely

2 tbsp. chopped fresh flat-leaf parsley

2 tbsp. chopped fresh mint

12 oz. dried rigatoni or other tubular pasta

12 large uncooked shrimp*

1 oz. unsalted butter

salt and pepper

Overleaf *Vineyards are very much part of rural Italy*

1 Fill a bowl with cold water and add the lemon juice. Prepare the artichokes one at a time. Cut off the stems and trim away any tough outer leaves. Cut across the tops of the leaves. Slice in half lengthwise and remove the central fibrous chokes, then cut lengthwise into ¼-inch thick slices. Immediately place the slices in the bowl of acidulated water to prevent discoloration.

2 Heat 5 tablespoons of the olive oil in a heavy-bottom skillet. Drain the artichoke slices and pat dry with paper towels. Add them to the skillet with the shallots, garlic, parsley, and mint, and cook over low heat, stirring frequently, for 10–12 minutes until tender.

3 Meanwhile, bring a large pan of lightly salted water to a boil. Add the pasta, bring back to a boil, and cook for 8–10 minutes, until tender but still firm to the bite.

4 Shell the shrimp, cut a slit along the back of each, and remove and discard the dark vein. Melt the butter in a small skillet, cut the shrimp in half, and add them to the skillet. Cook, stirring occasionally, for 2–3 minutes, until they have changed color. Season to taste with salt and pepper.

5 Drain the pasta and pour it into a bowl. Add the remaining olive oil and toss well. Add the artichoke mixture and the shrimp and toss again. Serve immediately.

*cook's tip

The large Mediterranean shrimp, known as *gamberoni* in Italy, have a superb flavor and texture that is superior to that of the very big jumbo shrimp, but they may be difficult to obtain.

rabid pasta   87
pasta all'arrabbiata

The pasta is "arrabbiata"—rabid or angry—because it is red hot with fiery chilies. This dish is a speciality of the province of Lazio.

SERVES 4

for the sugocasa

5 tbsp. extra virgin olive oil

1 lb. plum tomatoes, chopped

salt and pepper

²/₃ cup dry white wine

1 tbsp. sun-dried tomato paste

2 fresh red chilies

2 garlic cloves, finely chopped

12 oz. dried tortiglioni

4 tbsp. chopped fresh flat-leaf parsley

salt and pepper

shavings of pecorino cheese, to garnish

1 First make the sugocasa.* Heat the olive oil in a skillet until it is almost smoking. Add the tomatoes and cook over high heat for 2–3 minutes. Reduce the heat to low and cook gently for 20 minutes, or until very soft. Season with salt and pepper, then pass through a food mill into a clean pan.

2 Add the wine, tomato paste, whole chilies, and garlic to the sugocasa and bring to a boil. Reduce the heat and let simmer gently.

3 Meanwhile, bring a large pan of lightly salted water to a boil. Add the pasta, bring back to a boil, and cook for 8–10 minutes, until tender but still firm to the bite.

The church at Capella

4 Meanwhile, remove the chilies and taste the sauce. If you prefer a hotter flavor, chop some or all of the chilies and return them to the pan. Check the seasoning at the same time, then stir in half the parsley.

5 Drain the pasta and pour it into a warmed serving bowl. Add the sauce and toss to coat. Sprinkle with the remaining parsley, garnish with the pecorino shavings, and serve immediately.

*cook's tip
If time is short, use store-bought sugocasa, available from most supermarkets and sometimes labeled "crushed tomatoes." Alternatively, you could use strained tomatoes, but the sauce will be thinner.

radiatori with pumpkin sauce
radiatori al sugo di zucca

Long, slow cooking results in a marvelous melding of sweet flavors in the pumpkin sauce in this southern dish.

SERVES 4

for the sauce

2 oz. unsalted butter

4 oz. white onions or shallots, chopped very finely

salt

1 lb. 12 oz. pumpkin, unprepared weight

pinch of freshly grated nutmeg

12 oz. dried radiatori

scant 1 cup light cream

4 tbsp. freshly grated Parmesan cheese, plus extra to serve

2 tbsp. chopped fresh flat-leaf parsley

salt and pepper

1 Melt the butter in a heavy-bottom pan over low heat. Add the onions, sprinkle with a little salt, cover, and cook, stirring frequently, for 25–30 minutes.

2 Scoop out and discard the seeds from the pumpkin. Peel and finely chop the flesh. Add the pumpkin to the pan and season to taste with nutmeg. Cover and cook over low heat, stirring occasionally, for 45 minutes.

3 Meanwhile, bring a large pan of lightly salted water to a boil. Add the pasta, bring back to a boil, and cook for 8–10 minutes, until tender but still firm to the bite. Drain thoroughly, reserving about ⅔ cup of the cooking liquid.

4 Stir the cream, grated Parmesan, and parsley into the pumpkin sauce and season to taste with salt and pepper. If the mixture seems a little too thick, add some or all of the reserved cooking liquid. Pour in the pasta and toss for 1 minute. Serve immediately, with extra Parmesan for sprinkling.

variation

Although traditionally made with pumpkin, you could also use butternut or acorn squash for this dish.

90

linguine with anchovies, olives, and capers
linguine alla puttanesca

This flavorful Neapolitan dish takes its name from the Italian word puttana, *meaning a prostitute, but no one seems quite sure why.*

SERVES 4

for the sauce

3 tbsp. olive oil

2 garlic cloves, chopped finely

10 anchovy fillets,* drained and chopped

scant 1 cup black olives, pitted and chopped

1 tbsp. capers, rinsed

**1 lb. plum tomatoes, peeled (see page 36), seeded, and
  chopped**

pinch of cayenne pepper

salt

14 oz. dried linguine

2 tbsp. chopped fresh flat-leaf parsley, to garnish

1 Heat the olive oil in a heavy-bottom pan. Add the garlic and cook over low heat, stirring frequently, for 2 minutes. Add the anchovies and mash them to a pulp with a fork. Add the olives, capers, and tomatoes and season to taste with cayenne pepper. Cover and let simmer for 25 minutes.

2 Meanwhile, bring a pan of lightly salted water to a boil. Add the pasta, bring back to a boil, and cook for 8–10 minutes, until tender but still firm to the bite. Drain and transfer to a warmed serving dish.

3 Spoon the anchovy sauce into the dish and toss the pasta, using 2 large forks. Garnish with the parsley and serve immediately.

*cook's tip

Salted anchovies have a much better flavor than canned fillets, but are not so widely available. If you can find them, soak them in cold water for 30 minutes, then pat dry with paper towels before using.

Although not a long-standing tradition, baking packages of mixed ingredients in the oven has now become a favorite Italian cooking technique. It is especially well suited to seafood, because it seals in the moisture and keeps it tender.

seafood pasta packages
spaghetti ai frutti di mare al cartoccio

SERVES 4

3 lb. 5 oz. crab, cooked freshly

2 tbsp. virgin olive oil

2 fresh red chilies, seeded and chopped finely

4 garlic cloves, chopped finely

1 lb. 12 oz. canned tomatoes

1 cup dry white wine

salt and pepper

12 oz. dried spaghetti

1 lb. live mussels

2 tbsp. butter

4 oz. prepared squid, sliced (see page 181)

6 oz. uncooked jumbo shrimp

3 tbsp. coarsely chopped fresh flat-leaf parsley

1 tbsp. shredded fresh basil leaves

1 Holding the crab upright with one hand, bang it firmly on the underside of the shell with your clenched fist to loosen the body. Then, with the shell toward you and still holding it upright, force the body away from the shell by pushing with your thumbs. Twist off and discard the tail. Twist off the legs and claws. Crack them open and remove all the meat.

2 Pull off and discard the gills—dead man's fingers—then split open the body down the center using a sharp knife. Remove all the meat, discarding any pieces of shell. Reserve all the shell and set the crabmeat aside. Carefully break up the larger pieces of shell with a meat mallet or the end of a rolling pin.

3 Heat 1 tablespoon of the olive oil in a large pan. Add half the chilies and half the garlic, then add the pieces of crab shell. Cook over medium heat, stirring

occasionally, for 2–3 minutes. Add the tomatoes with their can juices and the wine. Reduce the heat and let simmer for about 1 hour. Strain the sauce, pressing down on the contents of the strainer with a wooden spoon. Season to taste with salt and pepper and set aside.

4 Bring a large pan of lightly salted water to a boil. Add the pasta, bring back to a boil, and cook for 8–10 minutes, until tender but still firm to the bite.

5 Scrub and debeard the mussels under cold running water. Discard any damaged or broken ones or those that do not shut immediately when sharply tapped.

6 Heat the remaining oil with the butter in a large, heavy-bottom pan. Add the remaining chilies and garlic and cook over low heat, stirring occasionally, for 5 minutes, until softened. Add the squid, shrimp, and mussels, cover, and cook over high heat for 4–5 minutes, until the mussels have opened. Remove the pan from the heat and discard any mussels that remain closed.

7 Drain the pasta and add it to the seafood with the chili and tomato sauce, parsley, and basil, tossing well to coat.

8 Cut out 4 large squares of parchment paper or waxed paper. Divide the pasta and seafood between them, placing it on one half. Fold over the other half and turn in the edges securely to seal. Transfer to a large baking sheet and bake in a preheated oven, 350°F, for about 10 minutes, until the packages have puffed up. Serve immediately.

layered spaghetti with smoked salmon and shrimp
pasticcio di spaghetti con salmone affumicato e gamberoni

Now enjoying considerable popularity in fashionable restaurants in many cities both in Italy and elsewhere in the world, pasta and smoked salmon is quite a recent partnership. This is a special dish, but astonishingly easy to make.

SERVES 6

2¹/₂ oz. butter, plus extra for greasing

12 oz. dried spaghetti

7 oz. smoked salmon, cut into strips

10 oz. large jumbo shrimp, cooked, shelled, and deveined

1 quantity Béchamel Sauce (see page 79)

1 cup freshly grated Parmesan cheese

salt

1 Butter a large, ovenproof dish and set aside.

2 Bring a large pan of lightly salted water to a boil. Add the pasta, bring back to a boil, and cook for 8–10 minutes, until tender but still firm to the bite. Drain well, return to the pan, add 2 oz. of the butter, and toss well.

3 Spoon half the spaghetti into the prepared dish, cover with the strips of smoked salmon, then top with the shrimp. Pour over half the béchamel sauce and sprinkle with half the Parmesan. Add the remaining spaghetti, cover with the remaining sauce, and sprinkle with the remaining Parmesan. Dice the remaining butter and dot it over the surface.

4 Bake in a preheated oven, 350°F, for 15 minutes, until the top is golden. Serve immediately.

variation

This dish would also be delicious made with smoked halibut instead of the salmon and smoked mussels instead of the shrimp.

Narrow alley in Gubbio

spaghetti with clams
spaghetti alla vongole

SERVES 4

2 lb. 4 oz. live clams

³/₄ cup water

³/₄ cup dry white wine

12 oz. dried spaghetti

5 tbsp. olive oil

2 garlic cloves, chopped finely

4 tbsp. chopped fresh flat-leaf parsley

salt and pepper

equipment

1 square of cheesecloth

In Italy, this dish would be prepared with small, smooth-shelled clams, known as vongole, *but you can use other varieties, such as Venus clams. If fresh clams are not available, substitute 10 oz. of clams in brine, which are sold in jars.*

1 Scrub the clams under cold running water and discard any with broken or damaged shells or those that do not shut when sharply tapped. Place the clams in a large, heavy-bottom pan, add the water and wine, cover, and cook over high heat, shaking the pan occasionally, for 5 minutes, until the shells have opened.

2 Remove the clams with a slotted spoon and set aside to cool slightly. Strain the cooking liquid through a cheesecloth-lined strainer into a small pan. Bring to a boil and cook until reduced by about half and remove from heat. Meanwhile, discard any clams that have not opened, remove the remainder from their shells, and set aside.

3 Bring a large pan of lightly salted water to a boil. Add the pasta, bring back to a boil, and cook for 8–10 minutes, until tender but still firm to the bite.

4 Meanwhile, heat the olive oil in a large, heavy-bottom skillet. Add the garlic and cook, stirring frequently, for 2 minutes. Add the parsley and the reduced cooking liquid and let simmer gently.

5 Drain the pasta and add it to the skillet with the clams. Season to taste with salt and pepper and cook, stirring constantly, for 4 minutes, until the pasta is coated and the clams have heated through. Transfer to a warmed serving dish and serve immediately.*

*cook's tip
Don't be tempted to serve Parmesan for sprinkling: cheese really doesn't marry well with this pasta recipe.

Gondolas in Venice

98 saffron risotto
risotto alla milanese

The saffron (giallo) *in what is probably Italy's best-known rice dish is very eye-catching. Its delicate flavor makes it an ideal* primo, *or first course.*

1 Place the saffron in a small bowl and add the boiling water. Set aside to soak. Pour the stock into a large pan and bring to a boil. Reduce the heat and let simmer gently.

2 Melt 2 oz. of the butter in another large, heavy-bottom pan. Add the onions and garlic and cook over low heat, stirring occasionally, for 5 minutes, until softened. Add the rice and cook, stirring, until all the grains are coated and glistening.

3 Add the wine and cook, stirring constantly, until it has almost completely evaporated. Add a ladleful of the hot stock and cook, still stirring constantly, until all the stock has been absorbed. Continue cooking, stirring and adding the stock, a ladleful at a time, for about 20 minutes,* or until the rice is tender and all the liquid has been absorbed.

4 Add the saffron liquid, the remaining butter, and the Parmesan, and season to taste with salt and pepper. Cook for 1–2 minutes, until heated through, then serve immediately.

SERVES 4

pinch of saffron threads

4 tbsp. boiling water

5 cups chicken or vegetable stock

3 oz. unsalted butter

2 onions, chopped finely

2 garlic cloves, chopped finely

generous 1½ cups risotto rice

⅔ cup dry white wine

¾ cup freshly grated Parmesan cheese

salt and pepper

*cook's tip

It is essential to stir the rice constantly for at least the first 10 minutes of cooking in the stock, and it is safer to do so throughout the whole cooking time. However, as you become a more experienced risotto cook, you will recognize the "feel" of the rice and can stir frequently, rather than constantly, for the last 10 minutes.

risotto with four cheeses
risotto ai quattro formaggi

1 Pour the stock into a large pan and bring to a boil. Reduce the heat and let simmer gently.

2 Melt the butter in another large, heavy-bottom pan. Add the onion and cook over low heat, stirring occasionally, for 5 minutes, until softened. Add the rice and cook, stirring constantly, for 2–3 minutes, until all the grains are thoroughly coated and glistening.

3 Add the wine and cook, stirring constantly, until it has almost completely evaporated. Add a ladleful of the hot stock and cook, stirring constantly, until all the stock has been absorbed. Continue cooking, stirring and adding the stock, a ladleful at a time, for about 20 minutes, or until the rice is tender and the liquid has been absorbed.*

4 Remove the pan from the heat and stir in the Gorgonzola, Taleggio, fontina, and about one-quarter of the Parmesan until melted. Season to taste with salt and pepper. Transfer the risotto to a warmed serving dish, sprinkle with the remaining Parmesan, garnish with the parsley, and serve immediately.

This is a very rich primo that would probably be served at a special-occasion dinner or to guests. Taleggio and fontina are wonderful melting cheeses that give the dish its creamy consistency.

SERVES 6

4 cups vegetable stock

1¹/₂ oz. unsalted butter

1 onion, chopped finely

generous 1¹/₂ cups risotto rice

scant 1 cup dry white wine

¹/₂ cup Gorgonzola cheese, crumbled

¹/₂ cup freshly grated Taleggio cheese

¹/₂ cup freshly grated fontina cheese

¹/₂ cup freshly grated Parmesan cheese

salt and pepper

2 tbsp. chopped fresh flat-leaf parsley, to garnish

*cook's tip

There is a saying in Italy that for a perfect creamy risotto, the rice should just catch on the bottom of the pan. Nevertheless, it is important to use a heavy-bottom pan to prevent the rice from sticking and burning.

100

seafood risotto
risotto alla marinara

Every town in the rice-growing regions of northern Italy has its own speciality risotto—this is Venice's.

1 Shell the shrimp, reserving the head and shells, and cut a slit along the back of each and remove and discard the dark vein, then set aside. Scrub the mussels and clams under cold running water and debeard the mussels. Discard any damaged or broken shellfish or those that do not shut immediately when sharply tapped. Wrap the shrimp heads and shells in a square of cheesecloth and pound gently with a pestle or the side of a rolling pin, setting aside any liquid they may yield.

2 Place the garlic, lemon, mussels, and clams in a large, heavy-bottom pan and add the cheesecloth-wrapped shells and any reserved liquid. Pour in the water, cover tightly, and bring to a boil over high heat. Cook, shaking the pan frequently, for 5 minutes, until the shellfish have opened. Discard any that remain closed. Transfer the mussels and clams to a bowl and strain the cooking liquid through a cheesecloth-lined strainer into a measuring cup. Add water to the reserved liquid to make 5 cups.

3 Pour this liquid into a clean pan. Bring to a boil, then reduce the heat and let simmer gently.

4 Melt 1 oz. of the butter with the olive oil in another large, heavy-bottom pan. Add the onion and half the parsley and cook over low heat, stirring occasionally, for 5 minutes, until softened. Add the rice and cook, stirring constantly, for 2–3 minutes, until all the grains are coated and glistening.

5 Add the wine and cook, stirring constantly, until it has almost completely evaporated. Add a ladleful of

SERVES 4

8 oz. uncooked shrimp

8 oz. live mussels

8 oz. live clams

2 garlic cloves, halved

1 lemon, sliced

2$\frac{1}{2}$ cups water

4 oz. unsalted butter

1 tbsp. olive oil

1 onion, chopped finely

2 tbsp. chopped fresh flat-leaf parsley

generous 1$\frac{1}{2}$ cups risotto rice

$\frac{1}{2}$ cup dry white wine

8 oz. prepared squid, cut into small pieces (see page 181), or squid rings

4 tbsp. Marsala

salt and pepper

equipment

2 squares of cheesecloth

the hot stock and cook, still stirring constantly, until all the stock has been absorbed. Continue cooking, stirring and adding the stock, a ladleful at a time, for about 20 minutes, or until the rice is tender and all the liquid has been absorbed.

6 About 5 minutes before the rice is ready, melt 2 oz. of the remaining butter in a heavy-bottom pan. Add the squid and cook, stirring frequently, for 3 minutes, then add the reserved shrimp and cook for an additional 2–3 minutes, until the squid is opaque and the shrimps have changed color. Stir in the Marsala, bring to a boil, and cook until the liquid has evaporated.

7 Stir the squid, shrimp, mussels, and clams into the rice, add the remaining butter and parsley, and season to taste with salt and pepper. Heat through briefly and serve immediately.

102 rice and peas
risi e bisi

1 Pour the stock into a large pan and bring to a boil. Reduce the heat and let simmer gently.

2 Melt 2 oz. of the butter in another large, heavy-bottom pan. Add the shallots and pancetta or bacon and cook over low heat, stirring occasionally, for 5 minutes, until the shallots are softened. Add the rice and cook, stirring constantly, for 2–3 minutes, until all the grains are thoroughly coated and glistening.

3 Pour in the wine and cook, stirring constantly, until it has almost completely evaporated. Add a ladleful of hot stock and cook, stirring constantly, until all the stock has been absorbed. Continue cooking and adding the stock, a ladleful at a time, for about 10 minutes.

4 Add the peas, then continue adding the stock, a ladleful at a time, for an additional 10 minutes, or until the rice is tender and the liquid has been absorbed.

5 Stir in the remaining butter and season to taste with salt and pepper. Transfer the risotto to a warmed serving dish, garnish with Parmesan shavings, and serve immediately.

variation

You can substitute diced cooked ham for the pancetta or bacon and add it toward the end of the cooking time so that it heats through.

This famous and rather pretty dish is one of many risotti *from the Veneto.*

SERVES 4

4 cups chicken or vegetable stock

3 oz. butter

3 shallots, chopped finely

4 oz. pancetta or rindless lean bacon, diced

scant 1 1/4 cups rice

2/3 cup dry white wine

1 1/2 cups petits pois, thawed if using frozen

salt and pepper

Parmesan cheese shavings, to garnish

pizza turnover 103
calzone

A calzone is a kind of inside-out pizza with the filling on the inside of the crust. This is a traditional cheese and vegetable recipe, but you could use almost any favorite pizza topping.

SERVES 4

2 quantities Pizza Dough (see page 105)

all-purpose flour, for dusting

for the filling

2 tbsp. olive oil

1 red onion, sliced thinly

1 garlic clove, chopped finely

14 oz. canned tomatoes, chopped

¹/₃ cup black olives, pitted

salt and pepper

7 oz. mozzarella cheese, drained and diced

1 tbsp. chopped fresh oregano

1 Heat the olive oil in a skillet. Add the onion and garlic and cook over low heat, stirring occasionally, for 5 minutes, until softened. Add the tomatoes and cook, stirring occasionally, for an additional 5 minutes. Stir in the olives and season to taste with salt and pepper. Remove the skillet from the heat.

2 Divide the dough into 4 pieces. Roll out each piece on a lightly floured counter to form an 8-inch circle.

3 Divide the tomato mixture among the circles, spreading it over half of each almost to the edge. Top with the cheese and sprinkle with the oregano. Brush the edge of each circle with a little water and fold over the uncovered sides. Press the edges to seal.

4 Transfer the turnovers to lightly oiled baking sheets and bake in a preheated oven, 400°F, for about 15 minutes, until golden and crisp. Remove from the oven and let stand for 2 minutes, then transfer to warmed plates and serve.

cheese and tomato pizza

pizza margherita

With its red, white, and green ingredients—the colors of the Italian flag—this pizza was created to honor Queen Margherita. Although it is delicious with just this simple topping, it can also be used as a basis for more elaborate pizzas with extra ingredients.

SERVES 2

for the dough

1¹/₂ **cups all-purpose flour, plus extra for dusting**

1 **tsp. salt**

1 **tsp. active dry yeast**

1 **tbsp. olive oil, plus extra for brushing**

6 **tbsp. lukewarm water**

for the topping

6 **tomatoes, sliced thinly**

6 **oz. mozzarella cheese, drained and sliced thinly**

salt and pepper

2 **tbsp. shredded fresh basil leaves**

2 **tbsp. olive oil**

1 To make the pizza dough, sift the flour and salt into a bowl and stir in the yeast. Make a well in the center and pour in the oil and water. Gradually incorporate the dry ingredients into the liquid, using a wooden spoon or floured hands.

2 Turn out the dough onto a lightly floured counter and knead well for 5 minutes, until smooth and elastic. Return to the clean bowl, covered with lightly oiled plastic wrap, and set aside to rise in a warm place for about 1 hour, or until doubled in size.

3 Turn out the dough onto a lightly floured counter and knock down. Knead briefly, then cut it in half and roll out each piece into a circle about ¹/₄ inch thick. Transfer to a lightly oiled baking sheet and push up the edges with your fingers to form a small rim.

4 For the topping, arrange the tomato and mozzarella slices alternately over the pizza bases. Season to taste with salt and pepper, sprinkle with the basil, and drizzle with the olive oil.

5 Bake in a preheated oven, 450°F, for 15–20 minutes, until the crust is crisp and the cheese has melted. Serve immediately.

variation

For Pizza Napoletana, first spread each pizza base with 4¹/₂ teaspoons tomato paste, then top with the tomato and cheese slices. Arrange halved, drained, canned anchovy fillets in a pattern on top, season to taste with pepper, drizzle with olive oil, and bake as above.

106

four seasons pizza
pizza quattro stagioni

This pizza is divided into four sections, each with a different topping, to represent the four seasons. You can vary the toppings according to taste.

SERVES 2

1 quantity Pizza Dough (see page 105)

all-purpose flour, for dusting

for the tomato sauce

2 tbsp. olive oil

1 small onion, chopped finely

1 garlic clove, chopped finely

1 red bell pepper, seeded and chopped

8 oz. plum tomatoes, peeled (see page 36) and chopped

1 tbsp. tomato paste

1 tsp. soft brown sugar

1 tbsp. shredded fresh basil leaves

1 bay leaf

salt and pepper

for the topping

$2^{1}/_{2}$ oz. drained bottled clams or drained anchovy fillets, halved lengthwise, or cooked shelled shrimp

2 oz. baby globe artichokes or artichoke hearts, sliced thinly, or canned asparagus spears, drained

1 oz. mozzarella cheese, drained and sliced thinly

1 tomato, sliced thinly

$3^{1}/_{2}$ oz. mushrooms or pepperoni, sliced thinly

2 tsp. capers, rinsed

2 tsp. pitted, sliced black olives

2 tbsp. olive oil, plus extra for brushing

salt and pepper

1 To make the tomato sauce, heat the olive oil in a heavy-bottom pan. Add the onion, garlic, and bell pepper, and cook over low heat, stirring occasionally, for 5 minutes, until softened. Add the tomatoes, tomato paste, sugar, basil, and bay leaf, and season to taste with salt and pepper. Cover and let simmer, stirring occasionally, for 30 minutes, until thickened. Remove the pan from the heat and let the sauce cool completely.

2 Turn out the prepared pizza dough onto a lightly floured counter and knock down. Knead briefly, then cut it in half and roll out each piece into a circle about 1/4 inch thick. Transfer to a lightly oiled baking sheet and push up the edges with your fingers to form a small rim.

3 Spread the tomato sauce over the pizza bases, almost to the edge. Cover one-quarter with clams, anchovy fillets, or shrimp. Cover a second quarter with sliced artichokes, artichoke hearts, or asparagus spears. Cover the third quarter with alternate slices of mozzarella and tomato. Cover the final quarter with sliced mushrooms or pepperoni. Sprinkle the surface with capers and olives, season to taste with salt and pepper, and drizzle with the olive oil.

4 Bake in a preheated oven, 425°F, for 20–25 minutes, until the crust is crisp and the cheese has melted. Serve immediately.

variation

Other toppings, either used in combination or singly, could include: mixed seafood, such as shrimp, mussels, and squid rings; roasted Mediterranean vegetables, say eggplants, bell peppers, tomatoes, zucchinis, and red onions; exotic mushrooms and pine nuts; or hot pepperoni and chilies.

seafood pizza

pizza alla marinara

SERVES 2

1 quantity Pizza Dough (see page 105)

all-purpose flour, for dusting

virgin olive oil, for greasing and drizzling

1 quantity Tomato Sauce (see page 106)

8 oz. mixed fresh* seafood, including cooked shrimp,
  cooked mussels, and squid rings

1/2 red bell pepper, seeded and chopped

1/2 yellow bell pepper, seeded and chopped

1 tbsp. capers, rinsed

2 oz. Taleggio cheese, grated

3 tbsp. freshly grated Parmesan cheese

1/2 tsp. dried oregano

2³/4 oz. anchovy fillets in oil,
  drained and sliced

10 black olives, pitted

salt and pepper

1 Turn out the prepared pizza dough onto a lightly floured counter and knock down. Knead briefly, then roll out the dough into a circle about 1/4 inch thick. Transfer to a lightly oiled baking sheet and push up the edge with your fingers to form a small rim.

2 Spread the tomato sauce over the pizza base, almost to the edge. Arrange the mixed seafood, red and yellow bell peppers, and capers evenly on top.

3 Sprinkle the Taleggio, Parmesan, and oregano evenly over the topping. Add the anchovy fillets and olives, drizzle with olive oil, and season to taste with salt and pepper.

4 Bake in a preheated oven, 425°F, for 20–25 minutes, until the crust is crisp and the cheese has melted. Serve immediately.

*cook's tip

If you have to use frozen mixed seafood, make sure it is completely thawed first.

Bags of fresh mixed seafood, containing shrimp, squid rings, mussels, and other shellfish are available from the refrigerated sections of many supermarkets. They tend to have a better flavor and texture than frozen seafood.

MEAT & POULTRY

112 Meat and poultry dishes traditionally fall into two categories—those for the rich and those for the poor. The former used the best cuts of meat from animals raised on lush pastures, often steak and veal. The latter, which were eaten less frequently, had to rely on tenderizing poorer cuts by long, slow cooking techniques. Both are equally delicious.

Italians do not eat a great deal of meat in comparison with some of their neighbors, and this is a contributing factor to the healthiness of their diet. They are also frugal and little is wasted, so variety meats also form an important part of their meat intake. Liver is popular, especially tender calf's liver, and chicken livers are often used to top pasta or crostini. Kidneys, brains, and sweetbreads form several regional specialities and tripe is cooked everywhere. Oxtail, calf's head, pig's feet, and calf's foot all have a role in traditional dishes.

By far the most popular meat in Italy is veal, a passion that is shared by few other nations with such intensity apart from the French. It is eaten in every region and recipes are innumerable. Calves are slaughtered at different ages to produce meat with different qualities, the best and most expensive being the very young *vitello di latte*, mainly produced in Lombardy and the Piedmont. Veal is served in a variety of ways: as *scallopine* (scallops) and *piccate* (extra thin scallops); *osso bucco*, made with shin of

Nothing of the animal is wasted—that which is not used for roasts, casseroles, stews, ham, and bacon is converted into salami, cured meats, and sausages

veal, and as *vitello tonnato* (see page 143)—thinly sliced cold roast veal served with a tuna sauce.

As with many peasant cultures, owning a pig is a way of life for many Italians. Nothing of the animal is wasted—that which is not used for roasts, casseroles, stews, ham, and bacon is converted into salami, cured meats, and sausages. Variety meats are an important food source, and even the snout and the tail have

their uses. Fresh pork is cooked in various ways, from roasted loin to fillet in sweet-and-sour sauce.

Lamb is part of many southern Italian recipes and is an especially popular meat in Lazio, the area surrounding Rome. Like veal, the quality and character of lamb depends on the age at which the animal is

Ponte Vecchio on the River Arno, Florence

Italy's cured meats are famous the world over.
Cured ham and salami hang on this wall

slaughtered. The youngest, most tender and succulent is known as *abbacchio*. Roast lamb is traditional on Easter Sunday, but there are many recipes for chops and braised lamb.

Beef in Italy is extremely variable. Tuscan beef ranks among the finest in the world, but meat from the south is usually far less tender and lean, mainly because the animals are not primarily bred for food but for working on the farm. Meat sauces for pasta and meatballs are made from ground beef; rump and fillet steak are broiled; topside is sliced and rolled around a stuffing mixture; and less tender, cuts are braised or stewed. *Carpaccio* (see page 46) is a famous dish of very thinly sliced raw fillet of beef, served as an antipasto.

Chicken is a popular and inexpensive source of meat in almost every country in the world, and Italy is no exception. As a general rule, it is cut into serving portions or boned and cut into bite-size pieces before cooking, rather than roasted or braised whole. Most chicken in Italy is still free range.

Turkey, duck, and goose also appear in various forms, the last often cooked with fruit to balance the richness of the meat. Most chicken recipes are interchangeable with turkey.

Furred and feathered game has a long history in Italian cuisine and still plays an important role in the daily menus of the southern regions in particular. Italians have been keen hunters for centuries and many continue to exercise a blatant disregard for the off season. One result of this is the increasing rarity of wild boar, once a standard dish in Tuscany and Sardinia. Young boar are cooked in the same way as pork, and older specimens are marinated for as long as 24 hours before roasting or braising.

Narrow cobblestone streets wind through old town centers

Italians are enthusiastic about the robust flavor of wild squab. Because these birds can be quite tough, they are usually served braised or stewed. A classic Tuscan dish is marinated squab braised with tomatoes and olives. Domestic squab are raised on many farms and although their flavor is less robust, they are generally far more tender than wild birds, making them suitable for roasting.

cured meats and sausages

The versatile and near-ubiquitous pig is the source of wonderful hams, salami, sausages, and other cured meats. Many are still homemade in farmhouses, and an enormous range of the commercial products are prepared by time-honored methods. Virtually every region has its own specialities.

Prosciutto, for which Italy is world famous, is a salted, air-cured ham that is best eaten raw, often as an antipasto, although it can be briefly cooked and is an essential ingredient in *saltimbocca*. The best-known prosciutto, or Parma ham, is produced in a legally defined area around the city of Parma between the rivers Baganzo and Taro. It comes from pigs that have been fed on the whey produced during the process of making Parmesan cheese, which gives it a sweet, mild flavor. The ham is quite fatty, as the pigs are reared indoors and not allowed to roam freely. San Daniele in Friuli also produces a fine, air-cured prosciutto considered by some to have a better flavor than Parma ham. Because the pigs are kept outdoors, the flesh is usually leaner. Prosciutto is also produced in several other places. It should be sliced wafer-thin and eaten within a day of purchase to prevent it from drying out.

Prosciutto cotto is cooked ham. It has usually been boiled and may be flavored with herbs. It is widely used for sandwiches and snacks.

Rabbit and hare are stewed, braised, or cooked in many of the same ways as chicken, often served with fried polenta. Farmed rabbit has a more delicate flavor than wild specimens and is widely available. Hare, however, cannot be farmed and so always has a rich, gamey flavor. Both rabbit and hare are popular in sweet-and-sour sauce and are usually well marinated in red wine and herbs before cooking.

At one time, thousands of quail were shot as they migrated to Italy for the summer months, but now they have become something of a rarity. Most quail is farmed these days and has a milder but still gamey flavor.

Although technically classed as game, guinea fowl have been farmed throughout Europe for centuries. They are about the size of a small chicken and have a similar but stronger flavor. They can be cooked in many of the same ways, including stuffed and roasted, casseroled, and pot roasted.

Bresaola, a speciality of Lombardy, is the beef equivalent of prosciutto, best made from thinly sliced fillet, salted, then air-dried for several months. Cheaper bresaola is made from leg of beef and is less tender. Bresaola is less salty, with a more delicate flavor than ham, and is usually served as an antipasto with a little olive oil and lemon juice. Like prosciutto, buy it in wafer-thin slices and eat as soon after purchase as possible.

Pancetta is a kind of bacon made from salted and spiced belly of pork. Unsmoked pancetta is usually sold in round, rolled slices, and the smoked version is more often sold in thin strips. It adds a surprising depth of flavor to pasta sauces, casseroles, and stews and is one of the main ingredients of *spaghetti alla carbonara*. It is widely available from Italian delicatessens. Lean bacon makes a reasonable substitute, because pancetta is quite fatty.

Salami is cured pork sausage that may be eaten raw or used for pizza toppings. There are many different varieties and local specialities, with varying proportions of lean and fat meat and a selection of seasonings and flavorings. Among the most common is the fat-speckled *salame milano*, which includes ground beef as well as pork and is flavored with white wine, garlic, and pepper. It is mass-produced and not held in especially high regard. Parma's *salame di Felino*, on the other hand, is very lightly cured and has a delicate flavor that is particularly fine. It is also quite expensive. *Salame sardo*, from Sardinia, and *salame napoletano*, from Naples, are both spiced with red and black pepper. Tuscany's version, *salame fiorentino*, is flavored with fennel seeds.

Other cured meats are produced in many regions and one of the best-known and most instantly recognizable is mortadella from Bologna. This large, mild, smooth sausage should be made from pure pork, but cheaper versions may include all kinds of other meat and nonmeat products. Although it is naturally a pale pink color, studded with cubes of creamy fat, avoid brilliant pink mortadella, which will have been colored artificially. Mortadella is nearly always eaten cold in sandwiches or as part of an antipasto, but it may be diced and added to pasta sauces and risotto.

Bologna is the city most associated with Italian cooking sausages, although they are produced in an immense variety in every region of the country. In addition to mass-produced sausages, there are also many small sausage stores, selling their own varieties flavored with local produce from fresh herbs to exotic mushrooms. Most sausages are made from coarsely chopped pork that is high in fat, but the speciality ones may be made from venison or wild boar.

Coppa, a dried and salted shoulder of pork sausage, is a speciality of Emilia-Romagna and Lombardy. It is irregular in shape, although tending toward the rectangular, deep red in color, and cased in natural skin. In Rome, the term *coppa* refers to a kind of meat mixture made from cooked pig's head rather than a sausage.

Cotechino is a lightly spiced and salted pork sausage from Lombardy, Emilia-Romagna and the Veneto. Weighing 2 lb. 4 oz., it is a large sausage cased in a skin—*coteca* means skin. It is an essential ingredient in *bollito misto* (see page 122) and is also served boiled and sliced with beans or lentils.

Luganega, from northern Italy, is a long, coiled pork sausage that is sold by length. It may be broiled or pan-fried and served with mashed potatoes or lentils. It can also be cut into chunks and stirred into risotto.

Zampone, often an ingredient in *bollito misto*, is a stuffed pig's foot, weighing 3$\frac{1}{2}$ to 4$\frac{1}{2}$ lb. When it is bought raw it needs to be boiled at home for 2–3 hours, or it can be purchased partially cooked and vacuum-packed. Zampone is sliced before serving with lentils or mashed potato.

Overleaf *A typical old Italian town illuminated at night*

meatball surprise
polpette sorpresa

The surprise is that the meatballs are stuffed with creamy melted fontina cheese. You can serve them in the traditional way with ribbon pasta, but children love them with French fries.

SERVES 8

1 lb. 2 oz. ground steak

1 lb. 2 oz. ground pork

2 garlic cloves, chopped finely

1 cup fresh bread crumbs

scant $^1/_2$ cup freshly grated Parmesan cheese

1 tsp. dried oregano

$^1/_2$ tsp. ground cinnamon

grated rind and juice of 1 lemon

2 eggs, beaten lightly

$5^1/_2$ oz. fontina cheese

6 tbsp. virgin olive oil

$1^1/_4$ cups dried, uncolored bread crumbs

salt and pepper

fresh flat-leaf parsley sprigs, to garnish

homemade Tomato Sauce (see page 106) or
  store-bought tomato sauce, to serve

1 Combine the steak, pork, garlic, fresh bread crumbs, Parmesan, oregano, cinnamon, and lemon rind in a bowl. Stir in the lemon juice and beaten eggs, season with salt and pepper, and mix well.

2 Knead the mixture with dampened hands, then shape small quantities into 16 balls.

3 Cut the fontina into 16 cubes and press 1 cube into each meatball, then reshape them to enclose the cheese completely.

4 Heat the olive oil in a large, heavy-bottom skillet. Meanwhile, spread out the dried bread crumbs on a shallow plate and roll the meatballs in them to coat.

5 Add the meatballs, in batches, to the skillet and cook until golden brown all over. Transfer to an ovenproof dish using a slotted spoon and bake in a preheated oven, 350°F, for 15–20 minutes, until cooked through. Serve immediately, garnished with parsley sprigs and accompanied with tomato sauce.

The Italian lakes draw many tourists during summer, but out of season the waters are more tranquil

122

mixed meat stew
bollito misto

The Italian name of this famous stew, which originated in the Piedmont, literally means a "boiled mix." There are numerous variations on the theme. Chicken, veal knuckle, and topside of beef are usually included, but cooks may also include pig's feet (zampone) or calf's head. You will need a huge pan, but this is a perfect dish for entertaining.

SERVES 8–10

1 veal knuckle

4 lb. chicken

1 lb. 9 oz. topside of beef

6 black peppercorns

2 bay leaves

1 tbsp. shredded fresh basil leaves

2 tsp. fresh thyme leaves

small white cabbage, quartered, thick stem removed

2 celery stalks, chopped coarsely

2 leeks, chopped coarsely

1 lb. carrots, sliced

12 baby white onions or shallots

2 lb. 4 oz. potatoes, sliced

1 cotechino or a 8- to 12-in. piece of other continental cooking sausage, such as luganega

to serve

gherkins

pickled pearl onions

mostarda di Cremona (optional)

green salad

1 Place the veal knuckle in a very large, heavy-bottom pan. Half-fill the pan with water, add a good pinch of salt, and bring to a boil. Skim off any scum that rises to the surface, then boil for 45 minutes.

2 Add the chicken, beef, peppercorns, bay leaves, basil, and thyme to the pan, cover, reduce the heat, and let simmer for 1½ hours.

3 Add the cabbage, celery, leeks, carrots, onions or shallots, potatoes, and sausage to the pan. If necessary, add more water to cover the vegetables. Bring back to a boil over medium heat, then reduce the heat and let simmer for an additional hour, until the meat and vegetables are tender. Check the seasoning and adjust if necessary.

4 Remove and discard the veal knuckle and the bay leaves. Transfer the beef, chicken, and cotechino to a cutting board. Carve the beef into slices and cut the chicken into pieces. Slice the sausage into bite-size pieces. Arrange all the meat down the center of a warmed serving platter.

5 Using a slotted spoon, arrange the vegetables around the meat. Spoon 4–5 tablespoons of the cooking liquid* over the meat and serve immediately with gherkins, pickled pearl onions, *mostarda di Cremona* if using, and a green salad.

*cook's tip
The richly flavored cooking liquid is traditionally served on its own as a separate soup course.

beef in red wine
stufato alla fiorentina

Apart from producing what is arguably the best olive oil in the world, Tuscany is renowned for producing quite simple dishes in which the flavors are perfectly harmonized. This is one of them.

SERVES 4

2 lb. 12 oz. topside of beef

salt and pepper

3 tbsp. olive oil

1 red onion, chopped

1 garlic clove, chopped finely

2 carrots, sliced

2 celery stalks, sliced

1¼ cups Chianti

7 oz. canned tomatoes, chopped

1 tbsp. chopped fresh oregano

1 tbsp. chopped fresh flat-leaf parsley

1 bay leaf

1 Season the beef all over with salt and pepper. Heat the olive oil in a large, flameproof casserole. Add the beef and cook over medium heat, turning frequently, until browned on all sides. Use 2 large forks to remove the beef from the casserole.

2 Reduce the heat, add the onion, garlic, carrots, and celery, and cook, stirring occasionally, for 5 minutes, until softened. Pour in the wine and add the tomatoes, oregano, parsley, and bay leaf. Stir well to mix and bring to a boil.

3 Return the meat to the casserole and spoon the vegetable mixture over it. Cover and cook in a preheated oven, 350°F, spooning the vegetables over the meat occasionally, for 3–3¼ hours, until the beef is tender.

4 Transfer the beef to a carving board and cover with foil. Place the casserole on high heat and bring the juices to a boil. Continue to boil until reduced and thickened.

5 Carve the beef into slices and place on a warmed serving platter. Strain the thickened cooking juices over the beef and serve immediately.

broiled steak with tomatoes and garlic

bistecca alla pizzaiola

Originating in Naples, where it is difficult to find any dish that does not feature the brilliantly colored, rich-tasting tomatoes of the region, this way of serving steak is now popular throughout Italy—and beyond.

SERVES 4

3 tbsp. olive oil, plus extra for brushing

1 lb. 9 oz. tomatoes, peeled (see page 36)
  and chopped

1 red bell pepper, seeded and chopped

1 onion, chopped

2 garlic cloves, chopped finely

1 tbsp. chopped fresh flat-leaf parsley

1 tsp. dried oregano

1 tsp. sugar

salt and pepper

4 6-oz. entrecôte or rump steaks

1 Place the oil, tomatoes, red bell pepper, onion, garlic, parsley, oregano, and sugar in a heavy-bottom pan and season to taste with salt and pepper. Bring to a boil, reduce the heat, and let simmer for 15 minutes.

2 Meanwhile, trim any fat around the outsides of the steaks. Season each generously with pepper (but no salt) and brush with olive oil. Cook under a preheated broiler according to taste: 2–3 minutes each side for rare; 3–4 minutes each side for medium; 4–5 minutes on each side for well done.

3 Transfer the steaks to warmed individual plates and spoon the sauce over them. Serve immediately.

pork fillets with fennel 129
scaloppine di maiale con finocchio

This is a very rich dish with a creamy Gorgonzola sauce that perfectly balances the aniseed flavor of the fennel and sambuca.

SERVES 4

1 lb. pork fillet

2–3 tbsp. virgin olive oil

2 tbsp. sambuca (see page 164)

1 large fennel bulb, sliced, fronds reserved

3 oz. Gorgonzola cheese, crumbled

2 tbsp. light cream

1 tbsp. chopped fresh sage

1 tbsp. chopped fresh thyme

salt and pepper

1 Trim any fat from the pork and cut into ¼-inch-thick slices. Place the slices between 2 sheets of plastic wrap and beat with the flat end of a meat mallet or with a rolling pin to flatten slightly.

2 Heat 2 tablespoons of the oil in a heavy-bottom skillet and add the pork, in batches.* Cook over medium heat for 2–3 minutes on each side, until tender. Remove from the skillet and keep warm. Cook the remaining batches, adding more oil if necessary.

3 Stir the sambuca into the skillet, increase the heat, and cook, stirring constantly and scraping up the glazed bits from the bottom. Add the fennel and cook, stirring and turning frequently, for 3 minutes. Remove from the skillet and keep warm.

4 Reduce the heat, add the Gorgonzola and cream, and cook, stirring constantly, until smooth. Remove the skillet from the heat, stir in the sage and thyme, and season to taste with salt and pepper.

5 Divide the pork and fennel between 4 warmed individual serving plates and pour over the sauce. Garnish with the reserved fennel fronds and serve immediately.

*cook's tip
Do not overcrowd the skillet when cooking the pork in step 2.

Rolling plains provide rich farmland for crops and grazing

130 pan-fried pork with mozzarella
scaloppine di maiale alla romana

SERVES 4

1 lb. loin of pork

2–3 garlic cloves, chopped finely

6 oz. mozzarella di bufala, drained

salt and pepper

12 slices prosciutto

12 fresh sage leaves

2 oz. unsalted butter

mostarda di Verona,* to serve (optional)

to garnish

flat-leaf parsley sprigs

lemon slices

equipment

toothpicks

Although many cities are snapping at Rome's heels for the title of gastronomic capital of Italy, the Eternal City still wears the crown.

1 Trim any excess fat from the meat, then slice it crosswise into 12 pieces, each about 1 inch thick. Stand each piece on end and beat with the flat end of a meat mallet or the side of a rolling pin until thoroughly flattened. Rub each piece all over with garlic, transfer to a plate, and cover with plastic wrap. Set aside in a cool place for 30 minutes to 1 hour.

2 Cut the mozzarella into 12 slices. Season the pork to taste with salt and pepper, then place a slice of cheese on top of each slice of meat. Top with a slice of prosciutto, letting it fall in folds. Place a sage leaf on each portion and secure with a toothpick.

3 Melt the butter in a large, heavy-bottom skillet. Add the pork, in batches if necessary, and cook for 2–3 minutes on each side, until the meat is tender and the cheese has melted. Remove with a slotted spoon and keep warm while you cook the remaining batch.

4 Remove and discard the toothpicks. Transfer the pork to 4 warmed individual plates, garnish with parsley and lemon slices, and serve immediately with *mostarda di Verona*.

*cook's tip

Mostarda di Verona is made with apple purée and is available from some good Italian delicatessens.

Left *Bicycles in Milan*

Overleaf *A patchwork of rooftops, Venice*

sausages with cranberry beans

luganega e fagioli

These mildly spiced pork sausages are made all over Italy, but the best are said to come from Lombardy, although the Veneto also produces vast quantities.

SERVES 4

2 tbsp. virgin olive oil

1 lb. 2 oz. luganega or other Italian sausage

5 oz. smoked pancetta or lean bacon, diced

2 red onions, chopped

2 garlic cloves, chopped finely

1 1/3 cups dried cranberry beans, covered and soaked
  overnight in cold water

2 tsp. finely chopped fresh rosemary

2 tsp. chopped fresh sage

1 1/4 cups dry white wine

salt and pepper

fresh rosemary sprigs, to garnish

crusty bread, to serve

1 Heat the oil in a flameproof casserole. Add the sausages and cook over low heat, turning frequently, for about 10 minutes, until browned all over. Remove from the casserole and set aside.

2 Add the pancetta to the casserole, increase the heat to medium and cook, stirring frequently, for 5 minutes, or until golden brown. Remove with a slotted spoon and set aside.

3 Add the onions to the casserole and cook over low heat, stirring occasionally, for 5 minutes, until softened. Add the garlic and cook for an additional 2 minutes.

4 Drain the beans and set aside the soaking liquid. Add the beans to the casserole, then return the sausages and pancetta. Gently stir in the herbs and pour in the wine. Measure the reserved soaking liquid and add 1 1/4 cups to the casserole. Season to taste with salt and pepper. Bring to a boil over low heat and boil for 15 minutes, then transfer to a preheated oven, 275°F, and cook for 2 3/4 hours.

5 Remove the casserole from the oven and ladle the sausages and beans onto 4 warmed serving plates. Garnish with the rosemary sprigs and serve immediately with crusty bread.

*cook's tip
The bittersweet flavor of cranberry beans makes a perfect contrast to the spiciness of the sausages and the smoky pancetta, but other beans, such as cannellini, would work well too.

136 slow-roasted pork
arrosto alla perugina

This wonderfully succulent roast from Perugia may be served hot with green beans or peperonata *(see page 205) or cold with a crisp salad.*

SERVES 6

3 lb. 8 oz. loin of pork, boned and rolled*

4 garlic cloves, sliced thinly lengthwise

1¹/₂ tsp. finely chopped fresh fennel fronds
  or ¹/₂ tsp. dried fennel

4 cloves

salt and pepper

1¹/₄ cups dry white wine

1¹/₄ cups water

1 Use a small, sharp knife to make incisions all over the pork, opening them out slightly to make little pockets. Place the garlic slices in a small strainer and rinse under cold running water to moisten. Spread out the fennel on a saucer and roll the garlic slices in it to coat. Slide the garlic slices and the cloves into the pockets in the pork. Season the meat all over with salt and pepper.

2 Place the pork in a large ovenproof dish or roasting pan. Pour in the wine and water. Cook in a preheated oven, 300°F, basting the meat occasionally, for 2¹/₂–2³/₄ hours, until the pork is tender but still quite moist.

3 If you are serving the pork hot, transfer it to a carving board and cut into slices. If you are serving it cold, let it cool completely in the cooking juices before removing and slicing.

*cook's tip

Prepared boned and rolled loin of pork is available from supermarkets and butchers, or you can ask your butcher to prepare one especially for you.

Like Abruzzi, Basilicata, located in the arch of Italy's "boot," uses the fiery hot, dried peperoncino chilies to flavor the specialities of the region.

spicy lamb with black olives
agnello alla basilicata

SERVES 6

6 tbsp. olive oil

1 onion, chopped

2 garlic cloves, chopped finely

2 lb. 12 oz. boneless leg of lamb, cut into
    1-inch cubes

2 dried whole peperoncini* or other red chilies

³/₄ cup dry white wine

1 cup black olives, pitted

2 tbsp. chopped fresh flat-leaf parsley,
    plus extra to garnish

salt

1 Heat the olive oil in a large, flameproof casserole. Add the onion and garlic and cook over low heat, stirring occasionally, for 5 minutes, until softened.

2 Add the cubed lamb and cook, stirring frequently, for 5 minutes, until browned all over. Crumble in the chilies, pour in the wine, and cook for an additional 5 minutes. Stir in the olives and parsley and season to taste with salt.

3 Transfer the casserole to a preheated oven, 350°F, and cook for 1½ hours, until the lamb is tender. Garnish with extra parsley and serve immediately.

*cook's tip

Peperoncini are not nicknamed "little devils" without good reason, so if you prefer a milder flavor, halve the quantity or use a variety of chili with less heat, such as ancho or choricero.

lamb shanks with roasted onions
agnello alla perugina

Slow-roasted lamb is infused with the flavors of garlic and rosemary and served with sweet red onions and glazed carrot sticks. You won't require anything more as accompaniment than a bottle of fruity red wine.

SERVES 4

4 12-oz. lamb shanks

6 garlic cloves

2 tbsp. virgin olive oil

1 tbsp. very finely chopped fresh rosemary

salt and pepper

4 red onions

12 oz. carrots, cut into thin sticks

4 tbsp. water

1 Trim off any excess fat from the lamb. Using a small, sharp knife, make 6 incisions in each shank. Cut the garlic cloves lengthwise into 4 slices. Insert 6 garlic slices in the incisions in each lamb shank.

2 Place the lamb in a single layer in a roasting pan, drizzle with the olive oil, sprinkle with the rosemary, and season with pepper. Roast in a preheated oven, 350°F, for 45 minutes.

3 Wrap each of the onions in a square of foil. Remove the roasting pan from the oven and season the lamb shanks with salt. Return the pan to the oven and place the onions on the shelf next to it. Roast for an additional 1-1¼ hours, until the lamb is very tender.

4 Meanwhile, bring a large pan of water to a boil. Add the carrot sticks and blanch for 1 minute. Drain and refresh under cold water.

5 Remove the roasting pan from the oven when the lamb is meltingly tender and transfer it to a warmed serving dish. Skim off any fat from the roasting pan and place it over medium heat. Add the carrots and cook for 2 minutes, then add the water, bring to a boil, and let simmer, stirring constantly and scraping up the glazed bits from the bottom of the roasting pan.

6 Transfer the carrots and sauce to the serving dish. Remove the onions from the oven and unwrap. Cut off and discard about ½ inch of the tops and add the onions to the dish. Serve immediately.

140 roast lamb with rosemary and marsala
agnello al rosmarino e marsala

Serving tender spring lamb on Easter Sunday to celebrate the end of the Lenten fast is traditional throughout the Mediterranean, including Italy.

SERVES 6

4 lb. leg of lamb

2 garlic cloves, sliced thinly

2 tbsp. rosemary leaves

8 tbsp. olive oil

salt and pepper

2 lb. potatoes, cut into 1-inch cubes

6 fresh sage leaves, chopped

⅔ cup Marsala

1 Use a small, sharp knife to make incisions all over the lamb, opening them out slightly to make little pockets. Insert the garlic slices and about half the rosemary leaves in the pockets.

2 Place the lamb in a roasting pan and spoon half the olive oil over it. Roast in a preheated oven, 425°F, for 15 minutes.

3 Reduce the oven temperature to 350°F. Remove the lamb from the oven and season to taste with salt and pepper. Turn the lamb over, return to the oven, and roast for an additional hour.

4 Meanwhile, spread out the cubed potatoes in a second roasting pan, pour the remaining olive oil over them, and toss to coat. Sprinkle with the remaining rosemary and the sage. Place the potatoes in the oven with the lamb and roast for 40 minutes.

5 Remove the lamb from the oven, turn it over, and pour over the Marsala. Return it to the oven with the potatoes and cook for an additional 15 minutes.

6 Transfer the lamb to a carving board and cover with foil. Place the roasting pan over high heat and bring the juices to a boil. Continue to boil until thickened and syrupy. Strain into a warmed gravy boat or pitcher.

7 Carve the lamb into slices and serve with the potatoes and sauce.

veal with tuna sauce

vitello tonnato

Veal is Italy's most popular meat and there are hundreds of different recipes, including this cold classic, which needs to be prepared the day before you serve it. If you can find only a rolled loin, you will need to unroll it before marinating.

SERVES 4

1 lb. 10 oz. loin of veal, boned

2 carrots, sliced thinly

1 onion, sliced thinly

2 celery stalks, sliced thinly

2 cloves

2 bay leaves

4 cups dry white wine

salt and pepper

5 oz. canned tuna, drained

4 anchovy fillets, drained and chopped finely

$^1/_2$ cup capers, rinsed and chopped finely

2 oz. gherkins, drained and chopped finely

2 egg yolks

4 tbsp. lemon juice

$^1/_2$ cup extra virgin olive oil

to garnish

lemon slices

fresh flat–leaf parsley

equipment

1 square of cheesecloth

1 Place the veal in a large, nonmetallic dish and add the carrots, onion, celery, cloves, and bay leaves. Pour in the wine and turn the veal to coat. Cover with plastic wrap and marinate in the refrigerator overnight.

2 Drain the veal, reserving the marinade, and roll the meat before wrapping it in a piece of cheesecloth, tying it with string so that it holds its shape. Place the veal in a large pan. Pour the marinade into another pan and bring to a boil. Pour it over the veal and add enough boiling water to cover. Season with salt and pepper, bring back to a boil, then reduce the heat, cover, and let simmer for 1$^1/_2$ hours, until tender but still firm.

3 Transfer the veal to a plate and set aside to cool completely, then let chill until ready to serve. Strain the cooking liquid into a bowl and set aside to cool.

4 Combine the tuna, anchovies, capers, and gherkins in a bowl or process in a food processor or blender to make a purée. Beat the egg yolks with the lemon juice in another bowl. Gradually beat in the olive oil, adding it drop by drop to start with and then in a steady stream. When all the oil has been incorporated, stir in the tuna mixture and about 2 tablespoons of the cooled cooking liquid to give the consistency of heavy cream. Season to taste with salt and pepper. Cover with plastic wrap and put in the refrigerator until required.

5 To serve, unwrap the veal and pat it dry with paper towels. Using a sharp knife, cut the meat into $^1/_8$– to $^1/_4$-inch-thick slices and arrange them on a serving platter. Stir the tuna sauce and spoon it over the veal. Garnish with lemon slices and parsley and serve.

milanese veal
osso bucco

This rich stew of veal, onions, and leeks is Milan's signature dish. It is traditionally served with Saffron Risotto (see page 98), known as risotto alla Milanese.

SERVES 4

1 tbsp. virgin olive oil

4 tbsp. butter

2 onions, chopped

1 leek, chopped

3 tbsp. all–purpose flour

salt and pepper

4 thick slices of veal shin (osso bucco)

1¼ cups white wine

1¼ cups veal or chicken stock

for the gremolata

2 tbsp. chopped fresh parsley

1 garlic clove, chopped finely

grated rind of 1 lemon

1 Heat the oil and butter in a large, heavy-bottom skillet. Add the onions and leek and cook over low heat, stirring occasionally, for 5 minutes, until softened.

2 Spread out the flour on a plate and season with salt and pepper. Toss the pieces of veal in the flour to coat, shaking off any excess. Add the veal to the skillet, increase the heat to high, and cook until browned on both sides.

3 Gradually stir in the wine and stock and bring just to a boil, stirring constantly. Reduce the heat, cover, and let simmer for 1¼ hours, or until the veal is very tender.

4 Meanwhile, make the gremolata by mixing the parsley, garlic, and lemon rind in a small bowl.

5 Transfer the veal to a warmed serving dish with a slotted spoon. Bring the sauce to a boil and cook, stirring occasionally, until thickened and reduced. Pour the sauce over the veal, sprinkle with the gremolata, and serve immediately.

variation

Modern versions of this dish often include tomatoes. If you like, add 14 oz. canned tomatoes with the wine and stock in step 3. You could also add in 1 finely chopped carrot and 1 finely chopped celery stalk with the onions and leek in step 1.

150

hunter's chicken
pollo alla cacciatora

Italians are enthusiastic hunters and this warming dish keeps them going even on the coldest day.

SERVES 4

½ oz. unsalted butter

2 tbsp. olive oil

4 lb. skinned chicken portions, bone in

2 red onions, sliced

2 garlic cloves, chopped finely

14 oz. canned tomatoes, chopped

2 tbsp. chopped fresh flat-leaf parsley

6 fresh basil leaves, torn

1 tbsp. sun-dried tomato paste

⅔ cup red wine

salt and pepper

8 oz. mushrooms, sliced

1 Melt the butter with the olive oil in a flameproof casserole. Add the chicken pieces and cook, turning frequently, for 5–10 minutes, until golden brown all over. Transfer the pieces to a plate, using a slotted spoon.

2 Add the onions and garlic to the casserole and cook over low heat, stirring occasionally, for 10 minutes, until golden. Add the tomatoes with the juice from the can, the parsley, basil leaves, tomato paste, and wine, and season to taste with salt and pepper. Bring to a boil, then return the chicken pieces to the casserole, pushing them down into the sauce.

3 Cover and cook in a preheated oven, 325°F, for 50 minutes. Add the mushrooms and cook for an additional 10 minutes, until the chicken is cooked through and tender. Serve immediately.

variation
Substitute Marsala for the red wine and add 1 green bell pepper, seeded and sliced, with the onion in step 2.

tuscan chicken
pollo alla toscana

Another robust casserole, which is good served with plenty of fresh crusty bread or ribbon pasta, such as tagliatelle, fettuccine, or tagliarini.

1 Place the flour on a shallow plate and season with salt and pepper. Coat the chicken in the seasoned flour, shaking off any excess. Heat the olive oil in a large, flameproof casserole. Add the chicken and cook over medium heat, turning frequently, for 5–7 minutes, until golden brown. Remove from the casserole and set aside.

2 Add the onion, garlic, and red bell pepper to the casserole, reduce the heat and cook, stirring occasionally, for 5 minutes, until softened. Meanwhile, stir the saffron into the stock.

3 Stir the tomatoes with the juice from the can, the sun-dried tomatoes, mushrooms, and olives into the casserole and cook, stirring occasionally, for 3 minutes. Pour in the stock and saffron mixture and the lemon juice. Bring to a boil, then return the chicken to the casserole.

4 Cover and cook in a preheated oven, 350°F, for 1 hour, until the chicken is tender. Garnish with the basil leaves and serve immediately.

SERVES 4

2 tbsp. all-purpose flour

salt and pepper

4 skinned chicken quarters or portions

3 tbsp. olive oil

1 red onion, chopped

2 garlic cloves, chopped finely

1 red bell pepper, seeded and chopped

pinch of saffron threads

²/₃ cup chicken stock or a mixture of chicken stock
  and dry white wine

14 oz. canned tomatoes, chopped

4 sun-dried tomatoes in oil, drained and chopped

8 oz. portobello mushrooms, sliced

²/₃ cup black olives, pitted

4 tbsp. lemon juice

fresh basil leaves, to garnish

lombardy duck
anatra alla lombardia

Rich meat, such as duck and goose, is combined with lentils in the cuisines of many countries, and Italy is no exception. This is a wonderfully flavorful dish that would be a good choice when entertaining because it can be prepared in advance and gently reheated.

SERVES 4

for the stock

1 celery stalk

1 garlic clove

6 peppercorns, crushed lightly

1 bay leaf

5 sprigs flat-leaf parsley

1 onion

1 clove

salt

5 lb. duck

1⅓ cups small brown lentils

1 tbsp. virgin olive oil

2 onions

2 celery stalks

2 tbsp. brandy or grappa

⅔ cup dry white wine

salt and pepper

1 tsp. cornstarch

1 Cut the duck into joints. Cut off the wings. Fold back the skin at the neck end and cut out the wishbone with a small, sharp knife. Using poultry shears or heavy kitchen scissors, cut the duck breast in half along the breastbone, from the tail end to the neck. Cut along each side of the backbone to separate the two halves. Remove the backbone. Cut each portion in half diagonally.

2 To make the stock, place the wings, backbone, and neck, if available, in a large pan and add the celery, garlic, peppercorns, bay leaf, and parsley. Stick the onion with the clove and add to the pan with a large pinch of

salt. Add cold water to cover and bring to a boil. Skim off any scum that rises to the surface. Then reduce the heat and let simmer very gently for 2 hours. Strain into a clean pan and boil until reduced and concentrated. Measure ⅔ cup and set aside all the stock.

3 Rinse and pick over the lentils, then place in a pan. Pour in enough cold water to cover and add the olive oil. Cut 1 onion in half and add with 1 celery stalk. Bring to a boil over medium heat, then reduce the heat and let simmer for about 15 minutes, until the lentils are just starting to soften. Drain and set aside.

4 Meanwhile, put the duck portions, skin-side down, in a heavy-bottom skillet and cook, gently shaking the skillet occasionally, for about 10 minutes. Transfer the duck portions to a flameproof casserole and drain off the excess fat from the skillet.

5 Finely chop the remaining onion and celery and add to the skillet. Cook over low heat, stirring occasionally, for 5 minutes, until softened. Using a slotted spoon, transfer the vegetables to the casserole.

6 Set the casserole over medium heat, add the brandy, and ignite. When the flames have died down, add the wine and the reserved measured stock. Bring to a boil, add the lentils, and season to taste with salt and pepper. Cover and let simmer gently over low heat for 40 minutes, until the duck and lentils are tender.

7 Combine the cornstarch with 2 tablespoons of the stock to make a smooth paste in a small bowl. Stir the paste into the casserole and cook, stirring frequently, for about 5 minutes, until thickened. Taste and adjust the seasoning, if necessary, and serve immediately.

FISH & SEAFOOD

Once an inexpensive source of food for all and a free source of food for those living on the coast, fish and seafood are fast becoming luxury items in Italy, as in other parts of Europe. It is just as well, then, that generations of Italian cooks have perfected the art of preparing and cooking them to bring out the full flavor of the sea and exploit their delicious texture.

Almost surrounded by sea and richly endowed with lakes and rivers, Italy has a venerable tradition of cooking fine fish. Freshwater catches include trout, carp, and perch, but eel is a special favorite. It may be cooked in a variety of ways, including broiling and stewing in wine. Virtually every region has its own version of a filling and tasty fish soup, from *burrido* in Sardinia to *cacciucco* in Livorno.

Marine pollution, however, particularly in the Mediterranean, but also in the Adriatic, together with the European scourge of overfishing, has depleted stocks. Nevertheless, the quality and variety of fish is awe-inspiring, but it now tends to be quite expensive.

Saltwater fish catches include some species not seen elsewhere. Sardines, although no longer common around the shores of their namesake Sardinia, can still be found in the Mediterranean, especially in the spring. About 4½–5 inches long, they are best cleaned, then broiled, baked, deep-fried, or barbecued when extremely fresh. Their oily flesh pairs well with spices, capers, and other robust flavorings. Salted or canned sardines are also used.

Sardines, although no longer common around the shores of their namesake Sardinia, can still be found in the Mediterranean

Anchovies do not travel well, so they are rarely seen fresh outside the Mediterranean. They are readily available canned in oil and are also preserved in salt, which helps retain their flavor, but in this form they are less seen outside Italy. Canned anchovies should be well drained and, if they are too salty for your taste, they can be soaked in a saucer of milk for 10 minutes, then rinsed and patted dry before use.

The salted version should always be rinsed well before use. Anchovies add a strong flavor to pasta sauces, such as *alla puttanesca* (see page 90), and are good on pizzas and in salads.

Swordfish is at the other end of the scale, ranging in size up to 16 feet long or more and weighing up to

The Grand Canal, Venice

158

1,100 lb. However, the fish is usually sold cut into steaks, which may be broiled, barbecued, baked in the oven, or cut into chunks and threaded onto skewers. The flesh can dry out easily, so it is best cooked with olive oil, tomatoes, and other classic Mediterranean ingredients.

Sicilian fishermen have been catching tuna for centuries. This large, oily fish, usually sold as fillets or steaks, combines superbly with robust Mediterranean flavors, such as olives and capers. In the past, the traditional Arab tuna hunt, the *mantaza*, resulted in a huge glut of fish, which inspired Ignazio Florio to can it. Preserved in oil, brine, tomato sauce, or any other, canned tuna is ideal for salads, sandwiches, vegetable stuffings, and snacks of all kinds.

Red mullet is a delicious fish with a delicate flavor, which is sometimes compared to that of shrimp. It can be broiled, baked, or cooked in a package—a favorite Italian method—and marries well with olives, olive oil, tomatoes, herbs, saffron, and garlic. Scaling red mullet is a time-consuming process, but worth the effort because it reveals the wonderful coloring. All Italians regard the liver as a delicacy, so it is not removed when the fish is cleaned.

The variety of sea bream found off the Italian shores is the gilt head. This is a relatively large fish, with delicate, flavorful, flaky white flesh. It is usually broiled or cooked in a package. For best flavor and texture, marinate the fish before cooking.

Sea bass has always been popular in Mediterranean cuisines, but it is only relatively recently that this fine fish has become fashionable elsewhere. The flesh is delicate and the fish is best broiled, pan-fried, or barbecued whole. It is also very good stuffed and baked in the oven. In Italy, sea bass is caught wild, but the farmed fish is widely available in other countries.

Venetians have an excellent supply of seafood, including shellfish not found outside of the lagoon

Canale Guidecca, Venice

Cod is a North Atlantic fish, but dried salt cod is extremely popular in several Mediterranean countries, Italy included. In this form it looks rather unappetizing —like a stiff piece of cardboard—and requires soaking for at least 24 hours, with several changes of water. It dates from the days before refrigeration when,

because it keeps well, it provided a good source of protein during winter months. In Italy, it is usually made into a paste or cooked in soups and stews.

A popular way to serve a selection of small fish— small fry—is to deep-fry them whole as *fritto misto di pesce* (see page 183). This can also be made from bite-size chunks of larger fish.

As well as octopus, squid, shrimp, clams, and

easily prepared and small specimens are best cooked quickly or they will become tough. Larger ones can be stewed slowly or braised in wine in the oven. All three creatures have ink sacs and may be cooked in this dark liquid, although that of octopus has a very pungent taste. Squid or cuttlefish ink is used to flavor and color fresh pasta. Served with polenta, squid in its own ink is a classic Venetian dish.

Italian mussels are now cultivated on ropes in pure seawater to avoid any possibility of pollution. Popular and inexpensive, they are sold by the liter. Italians like to steam open the mussels and then broil them on the half shell. Serve with tomato sauce or add them to pizza toppings, pasta sauces, or mixed seafood salads.

There are many types of clams in Italy, ranging from tiny smooth-shelled *vongole*, served with pasta, to razor shells and the large, ridged Venus clams. Because they tend to be rather full of grit, leave the clams in a large container of fresh water before cooking so that they disgorge any sand, etc. Clams can be prepared in the same ways as mussels, but may also be served raw, like oysters.

Shrimp play an important role in the cuisine around Italy's coasts, served simply as an antipasto, cooked as part of *fritto misto*, broiled and served in a creamy sauce or with mayonnaise, pan-fried with garlic and tomatoes, or coated and deep-fried. They range in size from tiny pink or brown shrimp, through delicately flavored medium-size *gamberelli*, to large, succulent *gamberoni*.

mussels, Italy's coastlines teem with an immense variety of other crustaceans and shellfish that are unfamiliar elsewhere. Cuttlefish are slightly larger and wider than squid and both have ten tentacles. Octopus is much larger and has, of course, eight tentacles. All of them taste quite similar, but octopus requires lengthy pounding to tenderize it before very long, slow cooking. Both squid and cuttlefish are

162
swordfish with olives and capers
pesce spada alla palermitana

SERVES 4

2 tbsp. all-purpose flour

salt and pepper

4 8-oz. swordfish steaks

generous ¹/₃ cup olive oil

2 garlic cloves, halved

1 onion, chopped

4 anchovy fillets, drained and chopped

4 tomatoes, peeled (see page 36), seeded,
  and chopped

12 green olives, pitted and sliced

1 tbsp. capers, rinsed

fresh rosemary leaves, to garnish

Swordfish is plentiful in the waters surrounding Sicily, where it is usually cooked with traditional Mediterranean ingredients. The recipe takes its name from Palermo, Sicily's main port.

1 Spread out the flour on a plate and season with salt and pepper. Coat the fish in the seasoned flour, shaking off any excess.

2 Gently heat the olive oil in a large, heavy-bottom skillet. Add the garlic and cook over low heat for 2–3 minutes, until just golden. Do not let it turn brown or burn. Remove the garlic and discard.

3 Add the fish to the skillet and cook over medium heat for about 4 minutes on each side, until cooked through and golden brown. Remove the steaks from the skillet and set aside.

4 Add the onion and anchovies to the skillet and cook, mashing the anchovies with a wooden spoon until they have turned to a purée and the onion is golden. Add the tomatoes and cook over low heat, stirring occasionally, for about 20 minutes, until the mixture has thickened.

5 Stir in the olives and capers and taste and adjust the seasoning. Return the steaks to the skillet and heat through gently. Serve garnished with rosemary.

Back street in Venice, with the campanile of a church in the background

164 roast sea bream with fennel
fragolino al forno

All sea bream—and it is quite a large family of fish—is delicately flavored and especially delicious when stuffed and roasted. If possible, try to obtain gilt head sea bream, known as orata *in Italy, for this recipe.*

SERVES 4

2¼ cups dried, uncolored bread crumbs

2 tbsp. milk

1 fennel bulb, sliced thinly, fronds reserved for garnish

1 tbsp. lemon juice

2 tbsp. sambuca*

1 tbsp. chopped fresh thyme

1 bay leaf, crumbled

3 lb. 5 oz. whole sea bream, cleaned, scaled, and boned

salt and pepper

3 tbsp. olive oil, plus extra for brushing

1 red onion, chopped

1¼ cups dry white wine

1 Place the bread crumbs in a bowl, add the milk, and set aside for 5 minutes to soak. Place the fennel in another bowl and add the lemon juice, sambuca, thyme, and bay leaf. Squeeze the bread crumbs and add them to the mixture, stirring well.

2 Rinse the fish inside and out under cold running water and pat dry with paper towels. Season with salt and pepper. Spoon the fennel mixture into the cavity, then bind the fish with trussing thread or kitchen string.

3 Brush a large ovenproof dish with olive oil and sprinkle the onion over the bottom. Lay the fish on top and pour in the wine—it should reach about one-third of the way up the fish. Drizzle the sea bream with the olive oil and cook in preheated oven, 475°F, for 25–30 minutes. Baste the fish occasionally with the cooking juices and if it starts to brown, cover with a piece of foil to protect it.

4 Carefully lift out the fish, remove the string, and place on a warmed serving platter. Garnish with the reserved fennel fronds and serve immediately.

*cook's tip

Sambuca is an Italian liqueur distilled from witch elder, but it has a strong aniseed flavor, which marries well with fish. If it is unavailable, substitute Pernod.

broiled sardines with lemon sauce
sarde al limone

Most traditional sardine dishes come from the south of the country where the waters once teemed with shoals of these small, silver fish. In recent years, stocks have suffered through the demands of the canning industry.

SERVES 4

1 large lemon

3 oz. unsalted butter

salt and pepper

20 fresh sardines,* cleaned and heads removed

1 tbsp. chopped fresh fennel leaves

1 Peel the lemon. Remove all the bitter pith and discard. Using a small, serrated knife, cut between the membranes and ease out the flesh segments, discarding any seeds. Chop finely and set aside.

2 Melt 1 oz. of the butter in a small pan and season with salt and pepper. Brush the sardines all over with the melted butter and cook under a preheated broiler or on a barbecue, turning once, for 5–6 minutes, until cooked through.

3 Meanwhile, melt the remaining butter, then remove the pan from the heat. Stir in the chopped lemon and fennel.

4 Transfer the sardines to a warmed platter, pour the sauce over them, and serve immediately.

*cook's tip

Sardines are delicious if they are very fresh, but quite unpleasant if they are not. If you are in any doubt about the freshness, use another small, oily fish, such as sprats.

fillets of sole in tomato and olive sauce

filetti di sogliole alla pizzaiola

Pizzaiola—*a mixture of tomatoes, garlic, and herbs—is usually associated with steak (see page 127) or pizza toppings, but it is also a tasty way of serving fish.*

SERVES 4

4 tbsp. olive oil

2 lb. plum tomatoes, peeled, seeded, and chopped (see page 36 for peeling)

2 tbsp. sun-dried tomato paste

3 garlic cloves, chopped finely

1 tbsp. chopped fresh oregano

salt and pepper

generous ¹/₂ cup all-purpose flour

4 sole,* filleted

3 oz. unsalted butter

²/₃ cup black olives, pitted

1 Heat the olive oil in a large, heavy-bottom pan. Add the tomatoes, tomato paste, garlic, and oregano, and season with salt and pepper. Stir well, then cover and let simmer, stirring occasionally, for 30 minutes, until the mixture is thickened and pulpy.

2 Meanwhile, spread out the flour on a plate and season with salt and pepper. Coat the fish fillets in the seasoned flour, shaking off any excess.

3 Melt half the butter in a heavy-bottom skillet. Add as many fillets as the skillet will hold in a single layer and cook over medium heat for 2 minutes on each side. Using a spatula, transfer the fillets to an ovenproof dish and keep warm. Cook the remaining fillets, adding the remaining butter as required.

4 Stir the olives into the tomato sauce, then pour it over the fish. Bake in a preheated oven, 350°F, for 20 minutes. Serve immediately, straight from the dish.

*cook's tip

Dover sole and lemon sole are totally unrelated fish. The former is the "true" sole with an incomparable flavor. It is also very expensive and is probably best cooked plainly. Lemon sole suffers by comparison because it is unlucky enough to share the name. However, it is a tasty fish in its own right and less expensive. It is the best choice for this recipe.

trout in lemon and red wine sauce

trote alla trentina

SERVES 4

4 trout, cleaned, heads removed

1 cup red wine vinegar

1¼ cups red wine

⅔ cup water

2 bay leaves

4 sprigs fresh thyme

4 sprigs fresh flat-leaf parsley, plus extra to garnish

thinly pared rind of 1 lemon

3 shallots, sliced thinly

1 carrot, sliced thinly

12 black peppercorns

8 cloves

salt

3 oz. unsalted butter, diced

1 tbsp. chopped fresh flat-leaf parsley

1 tbsp. snipped fresh dill

salt and pepper

Trentino is a mountainous region in the northeast of the country with an abundance of lakes and rivers and plentiful fresh fish. However, even in Italy, inexpensive, farmed trout is becoming popular. As farmed fish often lacks flavor, it benefits from marinating and cooking with a variety of other ingredients.

1 Rinse the fish inside and out under cold running water and pat dry on paper towels. Place them in a single layer in a nonmetallic dish. Pour the vinegar into a small pan and bring to a boil, then pour it over the fish. Set aside to marinate for 30 minutes.

2 Pour the wine and water into a pan, add the bay leaves, thyme sprigs, parsley sprigs, lemon rind, shallots, carrots, peppercorns, and cloves, and season with salt. Bring to a boil over low heat.

3 Meanwhile, drain the trout and discard the vinegar. Place the fish in a single layer in a large skillet and strain the wine mixture over them. Cover and let simmer over low heat for 15 minutes, until cooked through and tender. There is no need to turn them.

4 Using a spatula, transfer the trout to individual serving plates and keep warm. Bring the cooking liquid back to a boil and cook until reduced by about three-quarters. Gradually beat in the butter, a little at a time, until fully incorporated. Stir in the chopped parsley and dill and taste; adjust the seasoning if necessary. Pour the sauce over the fish, garnish with parsley sprigs, and serve immediately.

170
beans with tuna
fagioli al tonno

This is a truly mouthwatering dish that has been horribly corrupted by cheap trattorie *that are no more Italian than a sushi bar. Forget any ghastly memories of canned beans and tuna and try the real thing. For hungry people you might allow 1 tuna steak each, but the beans are very filling.*

SERVES 4

1 lb. 12 oz. Great Northern beans, covered and soaked
  overnight in cold water

6 tbsp. extra virgin olive oil

2 7-oz. tuna steaks

2 garlic cloves, crushed lightly

sprig fresh sage

2 tbsp. water

salt and pepper

4 chopped fresh sage leaves, to garnish

1 Drain the soaked beans and place them in a pan. Add enough water to cover and bring to a boil. Reduce the heat and let simmer for 1–1½ hours, until tender. Drain the beans thoroughly.

2 Heat 1 tablespoon of the olive oil in a heavy-bottom skillet. Add the tuna steaks and cook over medium heat for 3–4 minutes on each side, until tender. Remove from the skillet and set aside to cool.

3 Heat 3 tablespoons of the remaining olive oil in a heavy-bottom skillet. Add the garlic and sage sprig and cook briefly over low heat until the sage starts to sizzle. Remove the garlic and discard.

4 Add the beans and cook for 1 minute, then add the measured water and season to taste with salt and pepper. Cook until the water has been absorbed. Remove and discard the sage sprig, transfer the beans to a bowl, and set aside to cool.

5 Meanwhile, flake the tuna, removing any bones. When the beans are lukewarm or at room temperature, according to taste, gently stir in the tuna. Drizzle with the remaining olive oil, sprinkle with the chopped sage, and serve.

variation

If you prefer to serve this dish chilled as an antipasto for 6, omit the olive oil in step 5 and make a dressing by putting 1½ teaspoons white wine vinegar, 1 teaspoon lemon juice, 2 tablespoons extra virgin olive oil, and salt and pepper to taste in a screw-top jar. Shake vigorously, pour over the beans and tuna, and toss lightly.

sicilian tuna
tonno alla siciliana

This quick, spicy dish can be cooked in the kitchen or on the barbecue. It needs nothing more than a crisp salad as an accompaniment.

SERVES 4

for the marinade

¹/₂ **cup extra virgin olive oil**

4 garlic cloves, chopped finely

4 fresh red chilies, seeded and chopped finely

juice and finely grated rind of 2 lemons

4 tbsp. finely chopped fresh flat-leaf parsley

salt and pepper

4 5-oz. tuna steaks

2 fennel bulbs, sliced thickly lengthwise

2 red onions, sliced

2 tbsp. virgin olive oil

crusty rolls, to serve

1 First, make the marinade by whisking all the ingredients together in a bowl. Place the tuna steaks in a large shallow dish and spoon over 4 tablespoons of the marinade, turning to coat. Cover and set aside for 30 minutes. Set aside the remaining marinade.

2 Heat a ridged grill pan. Put the fennel and onions in a bowl, add the oil, and toss well to coat. Add to the grill pan and cook for 5 minutes on each side, until just starting to color. Transfer to 4 warmed serving plates, drizzle with the reserved marinade, and keep warm.

3 Add the tuna steaks to the grill pan and cook, turning once, for 4–5 minutes, until firm to the touch but still moist inside. Transfer the tuna to the plates and serve immediately with crusty bread.

Right Gondolas have been used in Venice for over a thousand years

Overleaf Venice, view across the lagoon

red snapper with capers and olives

triglie alla calabrese

The delicately sweet flavor of the fish is deliciously complemented by the piquancy of the caper and olive sauce.

SERVES 4

1 lb. 9 oz. red snapper fillets (about 12)

3 tbsp. chopped fresh marjoram or flat-leaf parsley

thinly peeled rind of 1 orange, cut into thin strips

8 oz. mixed salad greens, torn into pieces

³/₄ cup extra virgin olive oil

1 tbsp. balsamic vinegar

1 tbsp. white wine vinegar

1 tsp. Dijon mustard

salt and pepper

3 tbsp. virgin olive oil

1 fennel bulb, cut into thin sticks

for the sauce

1 tbsp. butter

¹/₄ cup black olives, pitted and sliced thinly

1 tbsp. capers, rinsed

1 Place the fish fillets on a large plate, sprinkle with the marjoram, and season with salt and pepper. Set aside.

2 Blanch the orange rind in a small pan of boiling water for 2 minutes, drain, refresh under cold water, and drain well again.

3 Place the mixed salad greens in a large bowl. Whisk together the extra virgin olive oil, balsamic vinegar, wine vinegar, and mustard in a small bowl and season to taste with salt and pepper. Alternatively, shake all the dressing ingredients in a screw-top jar. Pour the dressing over the salad greens and toss well. Arrange the salad leaves on a large serving platter to make a bed.

4 Heat the virgin olive oil in a large, heavy-bottom skillet. Add the fennel and cook, stirring constantly, for 1 minute. Remove the fennel with a slotted spoon, set aside, and keep warm. Add the fish fillets, skin-side down, and cook for 2 minutes. Carefully turn them over and cook for an additional 1–2 minutes. Remove from the skillet and drain on paper towels. Keep warm.

5 To make the sauce, melt the butter in a small pan, add the olives and capers, and cook, stirring constantly, for 1 minute.

6 Place the fish fillets on the bed of salad greens, top with the orange rind and fennel, and pour over the sauce or pass it around separately in a warmed pitcher. Serve immediately.

178 # red snapper cooked in a package
triglie al cartoccio

SERVES 4

4 tbsp. extra virgin olive oil, plus extra for brushing

4 10-oz. red snapper, cleaned and scaled,
   heads on

salt and pepper

4 garlic cloves, sliced thinly lengthwise

4 tomatoes, peeled (see page 36), seeded, and diced

2 tsp. finely chopped fresh rosemary

fresh bread, to serve

Red snapper is a popular fish in Italy, not just because of its wonderful taste but also because it looks so attractive. This is an ideal way of cooking it.

1 Cut 4 squares of waxed paper large enough to enclose the fish and brush with a little olive oil.

2 Rinse the fish inside and out under cold running water and pat dry with paper towels. Season. Using a sharp knife, cut 3 diagonal slits in both sides of each fish. Insert the garlic slices into the slits.

3 Combine the olive oil, tomatoes, and rosemary in a bowl. Spoon a little of the mixture onto each of the waxed paper squares, then place the fish on top. Divide the remaining tomato mixture between the fish.

4 Fold up the paper around the fish, twisting it into tiny pleats to seal securely. Place the packages on a baking sheet and bake in a preheated oven, 400°F, for 15 minutes.

5 Transfer the packages to warmed plates and cut off the folded edges of the packages. Serve with bread.

variations

Pompano can be used rather than red snapper.
Substitute chopped fresh fennel leaves for the rosemary and add two or three parboiled new potatoes to the packages.

180 stuffed squid
calamari ripieni

Squid can be tricky to cook properly. To avoid making it tough, it should either be cooked very quickly or stewed slowly on a very low heat in the Italian way.

SERVES 4

8 sun-dried tomatoes*

8 small prepared squid (bodies about
  5 in. long) (see page 181)

1¹/₂ cups fresh white bread crumbs

2 tbsp. capers, rinsed and chopped finely

2 tbsp. chopped fresh flat-leaf parsley

salt and pepper

1 egg white

olive oil, for brushing and drizzling

3 tbsp. dry white wine

lemon juice, for drizzling (optional)

equipment

toothpicks

1 Put the sun-dried tomatoes in a bowl and cover with boiling water. Set aside for 15–20 minutes.

2 Meanwhile, finely chop the squid tentacles and place in another bowl. Add the bread crumbs, capers, and parsley.

3 Thoroughly drain the tomatoes and pat dry with paper towels. Chop them finely and add to the bread crumb mixture. Mix thoroughly and season to taste with salt and pepper. Stir in the egg white.

4 Spoon the bread crumb mixture into the squid body sacs, pushing it down well. Do not fill them more than about three-quarters full or they will burst during cooking. Secure the opening of each sac with a toothpick so the stuffing will not ooze out.

5 Generously brush oil over an ovenproof dish large enough to hold the squid snugly in a single layer. Place the squid in the dish and pour in the wine. Cover with foil and bake in a preheated oven, 325°F, for about 45 minutes, turning and basting occasionally. Test with a fork to check if the squid is tender.

6 Remove from the oven and set aside to cool to room temperature. To serve, remove and discard the toothpicks and slice the squid into circles. Place on warmed individual plates and drizzle with a little olive oil and either the cooled cooking juices or lemon juice.

cook's tip

Use sun-dried tomatoes from a package, not bottled in oil, for this recipe.

squid with parsley and pine nuts
calamari all'amalfitana

The Amalfi coast of Campania in southern Italy comprises a continuous succession of resorts and fishing villages. Unsurprisingly, seafood plays a starring role in the local diet.

SERVES 4

1/2 **cup golden raisins**

5 tbsp. olive oil

6 tbsp. chopped fresh flat-leaf parsley

2 garlic cloves, chopped finely

1 lb. 12 oz. prepared squid,* sliced, or squid rings

1/2 **cup dry white wine**

1 lb. 2 oz. strained tomatoes

pinch of chili powder

salt

3/4 **cup pine nuts, chopped finely**

1 Place the golden raisins in a small bowl, cover with lukewarm water, and set aside for 15 minutes to plump up.

2 Meanwhile, heat the olive oil in a heavy-bottom pan. Add the parsley and garlic and cook over low heat, stirring frequently, for 3 minutes. Add the squid and cook, stirring occasionally, for 5 minutes.

3 Increase the heat to medium, pour in the wine, and cook until it has almost completely evaporated. Stir in the strained tomatoes and season to taste with chili powder and salt. Reduce the heat again, cover, and let simmer gently, stirring occasionally, for 45–50 minutes, until the squid is almost tender.

4 Drain the golden raisins and stir them into the pan with the pine nuts. Let simmer for an additional 10 minutes, then serve immediately.

*cook's tip

To prepare squid, rub off the thin mottled skin from the body. Pull the head and tentacles away from the body. As you do this, most of the contents of the body sac will come away too. Cut off and set aside the tentacles. Squeeze out and discard the beak, along with the head and intestines. Pull out and discard the transparent quill from the body sac and any remaining intestines. Thoroughly rinse the squid inside and out with cold running water, drain in a colander, then pat dry with paper towels.

deep-fried seafood
fritto misto di pesce

Like many seafood recipes, this popular dish comes from the Campania region of southern Italy. It invariably contains a mixture of white fish fillets and shellfish, but the precise ingredients will depend on the day's catch.

SERVES 4

for the batter

³/₄ **cup all-purpose flour**

salt

1 egg yolk

1 tbsp. olive oil

1 cup milk

2 egg whites

corn oil, for deep-frying

7 oz. white fish fillets, such as lemon sole, skinned and
 cut into strips

7 oz. angler fish fillets, cut into bite-size chunks

4 shelled scallops, with or without corals

8 oz. large cooked shrimp, shelled but with
 the tails intact

to garnish

sprigs fresh flat-leaf parsley

lemon wedges

1 First, make the batter. Sift the flour with a pinch of salt into a bowl and make a well in the center. Add the egg yolk and olive oil to the well and mix together with a wooden spoon, gradually incorporating the flour. Gradually beat in the milk to make a smooth batter. Cover and set aside to rest for 30 minutes.

2 Heat the corn oil in a deep-fryer to 350–375°F or, if using a heavy-bottom skillet, until a cube of day-old bread browns in 30 seconds.

3 Meanwhile, whisk the egg whites in another bowl until they form stiff peaks, then gently fold them into the batter.

4 Using tongs, dip the seafood, a piece at a time, into the batter to coat, then add to the skillet and cook for 3–4 minutes, until crisp and golden. Do not overcrowd the skillet. As each piece is cooked, remove it from the skillet and drain on paper towels. Transfer to a serving platter and keep it warm while you cook the remaining seafood. Garnish with parsley sprigs and lemon wedges and serve.

variation

Fritto misto can also be made with a mixture of meat, such as strips of skinless, boneless chicken breast, and vegetables, such as sliced eggplants, sliced zucchinis, and white mushrooms.

Originating in the Mediterranean port of Livorno, this glorious Tuscan stew is easily the equal of its better-known French cousin, bouillabaisse. Serve it in deep bowls.

livornese seafood stew 185
cacciucco

SERVES 8

1 lb. freshly cooked lobster

12 oz. prepared squid, sliced into rings (see page 181)

3 lb. red snapper or gurnard fillets, sliced thickly

2 lb. cod fillet, sliced thickly

2 lb. tilapia or angler fish fillets, sliced thickly

²/₃ cup virgin olive oil

2 onions, chopped

1 carrot, chopped

2 celery stalks, chopped

1¹/₂ cups dry white wine

9 cups water

14 oz. canned tomatoes

1 bay leaf

1 fresh red chili, seeded

1 ciabatta or baguette, cut into ¹/₂-inch slices

4 garlic cloves, sliced thinly

2 lb. live mussels

4 fresh sage leaves

salt and pepper

1 First, place the lobster, right side up, on a cutting board and cut in half lengthwise with a sharp knife. Lift out the tail meat from each half and remove the black vein with the point of a sharp knife. Thickly slice the meat. Break off the claws and crack them with the back of a heavy knife or a meat mallet. Remove the meat from the claws, breaking it up as little as possible. Set aside the pieces of shell. Season the lobster meat, squid, and fish fillets with salt and pepper and set aside.

2 Heat 4 tablespoons of the olive oil in a large, heavy-bottom pan. Add the onions, carrot, and celery, and cook over medium heat, stirring occasionally, for 5–6 minutes, until just starting to color. Add 1¼ cups of the wine, the water, tomatoes, bay leaf, chili, and reserved lobster shell. Bring to a boil, then reduce the heat and let simmer gently for 50 minutes.

3 Meanwhile, spread out the bread slices on a baking sheet and drizzle with 2 tablespoons of the remaining olive oil. Bake in a preheated oven, 400°F, for about 10 minutes, until crisp. Remove from the oven and rub each slice with 1 of the garlic cloves. Set aside until required.

4 Strain the stock, pressing down on the contents of the strainer with the back of a wooden spoon. Measure and set aside 5 cups.

5 Scrub and debeard the mussels under cold running water. Discard any damaged or broken ones or those that do not shut immediately when sharply tapped. Put the mussels in a large pan, add the remaining wine, cover, and cook over high heat, shaking the pan occasionally, for 3–5 minutes, until the shells have opened. Strain the mussels, reserving the cooking liquid, discarding any that remain closed.

6 Finely chop the remaining garlic. Heat the remaining olive oil in a large pan, add the sage leaves and chopped garlic, and cook for 1 minute. Add the squid and cook, stirring frequently, for 2–3 minutes, until golden. Remove the squid with a slotted spoon.

7 Add all the fish fillets and the stock to the pan and bring to a boil. Reduce the heat and let simmer for 5 minutes. Return the squid to the pan and add the mussels, lobster meat, and 2 tablespoons of the reserved cooking liquid. Let simmer for an additional 2 minutes, until heated through. Taste and adjust the seasoning, if necessary, then serve immediately with the garlic toasts.

186

seafood in saffron sauce
frutti di mare in salsa gialla

This Venetian seafood stew is packed with flavor and needs plenty of fresh bread to mop up the delicious broth.

SERVES 4

8 oz. live clams

8 oz. live mussels

2 tbsp. olive oil

1 onion, sliced

pinch of saffron threads

1 tbsp. chopped fresh thyme

salt

2 garlic cloves, chopped finely

1 lb. 12 oz. canned tomatoes, drained and chopped

³/₄ cup dry white wine

8 cups fish stock

salt and pepper

12 oz. red snapper fillets, cut into bite-size chunks

1 lb. angler fish fillet, cut into bite-size chunks

8 oz. squid rings

2 tbsp. shredded fresh basil leaves

1 Scrub the clams and mussels under cold running water and debeard the mussels. Discard any damaged or broken shellfish and those that do not shut immediately when sharply tapped. Set aside.

2 Heat the olive oil in a large, flameproof casserole. Add the onion, saffron, thyme, and a pinch of salt. Cook over low heat, stirring occasionally, for 5 minutes, until the onion has softened. Add the garlic and cook for an additional 2 minutes.

3 Add the tomatoes and pour in the wine and stock. Season to taste with salt and pepper, bring to a boil, then reduce the heat and let simmer for 15 minutes.

4 Add the snapper and angler fish and let simmer for 3 minutes. Add the clams, mussels, and squid rings and let simmer for about 5 minutes, until the shellfish have opened. Discard any clams or mussels that remain shut. Stir in the basil and serve immediately.

St. Mark's Square, Venice, with a view of the famous Byzantine Basilica and the Campanile

188
seafood omelet
frittata di frutti di mare

This substantial omelet makes a quick and easy midweek supper dish—a nourishing secondo *(second course) for a family meal. For a larger family, double the quantity and use two skillets.*

SERVES 3

2 tbsp. unsalted butter

1 tbsp. olive oil

1 onion, chopped very finely

6 oz. zucchini, halved lengthwise and sliced

1 celery stalk, chopped very finely

3 oz. white mushrooms, sliced

2 oz. green beans, cut into 2-in. lengths

4 eggs

³/₈ cup mascarpone cheese

1 tbsp. chopped fresh thyme

1 tbsp. shredded fresh basil

salt and pepper

7 oz. canned tuna, drained and flaked

4 oz. shelled cooked shrimp

1 Melt the butter with the olive oil in a heavy-bottom skillet with a flameproof handle. If the skillet has a wooden handle, protect it with foil because it needs to go under the broiler. Add the onion and cook over low heat, stirring occasionally, for 5 minutes, until softened.

2 Add the zucchini, celery, mushrooms, and beans and cook, stirring occasionally, for an additional 8–10 minutes, until starting to brown.

3 Beat the eggs with the mascarpone, thyme, basil, and salt and pepper to taste.

4 Add the tuna to the skillet and stir it into the mixture with a wooden spoon. Add the shrimp last.

5 Pour the egg mixture into the skillet and cook for 5 minutes, until it is just starting to set. Draw the egg from the sides of the skillet toward the center to let the uncooked egg run underneath.

6 Put the skillet under a preheated broiler and cook until the egg is just set and the surface is starting to brown. Cut the omelet into wedges and serve.

VEGETABLES & SALADS

192

By a quirk of history, the fruits and vegetables we most associate with Italy such as tomatoes, zucchini, and bell peppers are from the New World, and eggplant is from Asia. Intrepid explorers such as Christopher Columbus set forth from Europe into the unknown, and the new foods they brought back have been enhanced by Italian cooks who created the recipes.

Italians treat their vegetables with respect, almost reverence, rather than as an afterthought to accompany a main dish. Although a single, simply cooked vegetable may be served with the *secondo*, its role is more as a garnish than an accompaniment. Generally, vegetables form the basis of dishes in their own right, either baked, braised, or stuffed. They are selected with care, daily where possible, to be sure that they are in peak condition. Because locally grown produce is preferred, vegetable dishes have a distinctly regional character—if the best eggplant

grow in Calabria and Sicily, look to those places for the most interesting and tastiest ways of cooking it. Similarly, you could prepare a different Neapolitan dish every week of the year and probably still find new ways with tomatoes. Of course, many vegetables, from bell peppers to zucchini and from peas to onions, grow throughout the country and are widely used not only in vegetable dishes but also as flavorful additions to meat and fish stews and casseroles and for pasta sauces and stuffings.

Most vegetable dishes concentrate on one particular type, rather than a medley of different ones. Garlic and sometimes onions or tomatoes may be added for extra flavor, but if an Italian is preparing, say, braised fennel, then fennel has pride of place and it is cooked in a way to ensure that its own distinctive flavor and texture are dominant.

There are favorite methods of preparing vegetables that may be applied to several different types. For example, *in agrodolce*, a sweet-and-sour sauce made with wine and balsamic vinegars and sugar, is a popular way of cooking different vegetables, such as onions and globe artichokes. In fact, *agrodolce* is so delicious, its use extends to cooking meat, such as lamb and game.

Naturally, salads are part of the cuisine of a country with gloriously sunny summers, but in Italy, they have greater importance than as mere substitutes for a hot dish because of the weather. They are sometimes served as an antipasto, but equally often they are

introduced after the *secondo*, as a palate cleanser and a "breathing space." They may also be served as an accompaniment to a meat or fish dish. Simple green salads often appear on the menu, but usually include a greater variety of leaves than just lettuce: chicory, radicchio, arugula, baby spinach, and fresh herbs may all feature. However, salads are also made with a vast range of vegetables and other ingredients, including bell peppers, mushrooms, tomatoes, cheese, anchovies, onions, oranges, capers, and olives, although only a few, complementary flavors are combined in any one dish. A classic example of this is *insalata tricolore* (see page 220), a perfect mix of mozzarella cheese, sliced tomatoes and basil leaves.

Salads are usually dressed with a simple vinaigrette made with olive oil and vinegar or freshly squeezed

Italians treat their vegetables with respect, almost reverence, rather than as an afterthought to accompany a main dish

lemon juice. For the best results, select an extra virgin olive oil, which has the fullest and fruitiest flavor. An interesting variation is to use walnut oil, which used to be far less expensive than olive oil because walnut trees grew all over Lombardy and other parts of northern Italy. The walnut flavor goes well with robust, peasant-style salads, although sadly it is now an expensive oil, in Italy and elsewhere.

baked eggplant and tomatoes 197
melanzane e pomodori al forno

Eggplant is especially popular in the cooking of southern Italy and Sicily and combine superbly with tomatoes, which also grow so well in these regions.

SERVES 4

1 lb. 5 oz. eggplant, cut into
  ¹/₂ -in. thick slices
salt
1 lb. 5 oz. plum tomatoes, cut into
  ¹/₂-in. thick slices
1 cup olive oil
salt and pepper
¹/₂ cup freshly grated Parmesan cheese
2 tbsp. fresh white bread crumbs

1 To remove any bitterness, layer the eggplant slices in a colander, sprinkling each layer with salt. Stand the colander in the sink and let drain for 30 minutes. Meanwhile, spread out the tomato slices on paper towels, cover with more paper towels, and let drain.

2 Rinse the eggplant thoroughly under cold running water to remove all traces of the salt, then pat dry with paper towels.

3 Heat 2 tablespoons of the olive oil in a large, heavy-bottom skillet. Add the tomato slices and cook for just 30 seconds on each side. Transfer to a large platter and season to taste with salt and pepper.

4 Wipe out the skillet with paper towels, then add 2 tablespoons of the remaining olive oil and heat. Add the eggplant slices, in batches, and cook on both sides until golden brown. Remove from the skillet and drain on paper towels. Cook the remaining slices in the same way, adding more olive oil as required.

5 Brush a large ovenproof dish with some of the remaining olive oil. Arrange alternate layers of eggplant and tomatoes, sprinkling each layer with Parmesan cheese. Top with the bread crumbs and drizzle with the remaining olive oil.

6 Bake in a preheated oven, 350°F, for 25–30 minutes, until golden. Serve immediately.

Bernini's Colonnade in the heart of Rome

198 eggplant with mozzarella and parmesan
parmigiana di melanzane

This makes a delicious accompaniment to plainly cooked chicken, pork, or veal and can also be served with salad as a vegetarian main course for four people.

SERVES 6-8

3 eggplant, sliced thinly

salt

olive oil, for brushing

10½ oz. mozzarella di bufala, sliced

1 cup freshly grated Parmesan cheese

3 tbsp. dried, uncolored bread crumbs

1 tbsp. butter

sprigs fresh flat-leaf parsley, to garnish

for the tomato and basil sauce

2 tbsp. virgin olive oil

4 shallots, chopped finely

2 garlic cloves, chopped finely

14 oz. canned tomatoes

1 tsp. sugar

8 fresh basil leaves, shredded

salt and pepper

1 To remove any bitterness, layer the eggplant slices in a colander, sprinkling each layer with salt. Stand the colander in the sink and let drain for 30 minutes. Rinse thoroughly under cold running water to remove all traces of salt, then pat dry with paper towels.

2 Arrange the eggplant slices in a single layer on one or two large baking sheets. Brush with olive oil and bake in a preheated oven, 400°F, for 15–20 minutes, until tender but not collapsing.

3 Meanwhile, make the tomato and basil sauce. Heat the oil in a heavy-bottom pan, add the shallots and cook, stirring occasionally, for 5 minutes, until softened. Add the garlic and cook for 1 minute more. Add the tomatoes, with their can juices, and break them up with a wooden spoon. Stir in the sugar, and season to taste with salt and pepper. Bring to a boil, reduce the heat, and let simmer for about 10 minutes, until thickened. Stir in the basil leaves.

4 Brush an ovenproof dish with olive oil and arrange half the eggplant slices in the bottom. Cover with half the mozzarella, spoon over half the tomato sauce, and sprinkle with half the Parmesan. Mix the remaining Parmesan with the bread crumbs. Make more layers, ending with the Parmesan mixture.

5 Dot the top with butter and bake for 25 minutes, until the topping is golden brown. Remove from the oven and let stand for 5 minutes, before slicing and serving, garnished with the parsley.

parmesan pumpkin

201

zucca alla parmigiana

Pumpkin is a popular vegetable in some countries—including all regions of Italy—and virtually ignored in others. This rich dish will instantly convert those who have never tried it.

SERVES 6

2 tbsp. virgin olive oil

1 onion, chopped finely

1 garlic clove, chopped finely

1³/₄ cups strained tomatoes

10 fresh basil leaves, shredded

2 tbsp. chopped fresh flat-leaf parsley

1 tsp. sugar

salt and pepper

2 eggs, beaten lightly

¹/₂ cup dried, uncolored bread crumbs

3¹/₂ lb. pumpkin, peeled, seeded, and sliced

2 oz. butter, plus extra for greasing

¹/₂ cup freshly grated Parmesan cheese

1 Heat the olive oil in a large pan, add the onion and garlic, and cook over low heat for 5 minutes, until softened. Stir in the strained tomatoes, basil, parsley, and sugar, and season to taste with salt and pepper. Let simmer for 10-15 minutes, until thickened.

2 Meanwhile, put the beaten eggs in a shallow dish and spread out the bread crumbs in another shallow dish. Dip the slices of pumpkin first in the egg, then in the bread crumbs to coat, shaking off any excess.

3 Grease a large ovenproof dish with butter. Melt the butter in a large, heavy-bottom skillet. Add the pumpkin slices, in batches, and cook until browned all over. Transfer the slices to the dish. Pour the sauce over them and sprinkle with the Parmesan.

4 Bake in a preheated oven, 350°F, for 30 minutes, until the cheese is bubbling and golden. Serve immediately.

The skyline of Florence is like a view from a bygone age

202

sweet-and-sour onions
cipolline in agrodolce

SERVES 4

2 oz. unsalted butter

5 tbsp. white granulated sugar

2 tbsp. balsamic vinegar

$^1/_2$ cup white wine vinegar

1 lb. 7 oz. pearl onions

salt and pepper

This combination of sweet and sour is a favorite Italian way of cooking all kinds of foods, from vegetables, such as zucchinis and globe artichokes, to game, such as rabbit and hare. You can serve these onions as an accompaniment to roasts and broils or as part of an antipasti.

1 Melt the butter in a heavy-bottom skillet over low heat. Add the sugar and heat, stirring constantly, until it has dissolved.

2 Stir in the balsamic and white wine vinegars, then add the onions and season to taste with salt and pepper.

3 Increase the heat to medium, cover, and cook for 25 minutes, until the onions are tender and golden. Serve immediately.

This quick and easy accompaniment goes superbly well with broiled meat or fish.

braised zucchini
zucchini alla calabrese

SERVES 4

2 tbsp. olive oil

2 red onions, chopped

1 garlic clove, chopped finely

5 zucchini, cut into ¹/₂-in. thick slices

²/₃ cup vegetable stock

1 tsp. chopped fresh oregano

salt and pepper

1 Heat the olive oil in a large, heavy-bottom skillet. Add the onions and garlic and cook over medium heat, stirring occasionally, for 5 minutes until softened and starting to color.

2 Add the zucchini and cook, stirring frequently, for 4–5 minutes, until just starting to color.

3 Pour in the stock, add the oregano, and season to taste with salt and pepper. Reduce the heat and let simmer gently for about 10 minutes, until all the liquid has evaporated. Serve immediately.

variation
Add scant 1 cup diced pancetta or rindless lean bacon with the onions in step 1.

braised fennel
finocchi stufati

204

Slow braising is a traditional Italian way of cooking many vegetables, because it intensifies the flavor and also makes it more subtle.

SERVES 4

2 fennel bulbs

1 tbsp. olive oil

1 onion, sliced thinly

2 tomatoes, peeled (see page 36) and chopped

¹/₃ cup black olives, pitted

²/₃ cup vegetable stock

2 tbsp. torn fresh basil leaves

pepper

1 Cut off and chop the fennel fronds and set aside for garnishing. Cut the bulbs in half lengthwise, then slice them thinly.

2 Heat the olive oil in a heavy-bottom skillet. Add the onion and cook over low heat, stirring occasionally, for 5 minutes, until softened. Add the fennel slices and cook, stirring occasionally, for an additional 10 minutes.

3 Add the tomatoes and olives and pour in enough stock to cover the bottom of the skillet. Cover and let simmer gently for 20 minutes, until the fennel is very tender. Stir in the basil and season to taste with pepper. Transfer to a warmed serving dish, garnish with the reserved fennel fronds, and serve immediately.

variation
If you prefer your fennel crisper, omit the stock in step 3 and cook the fennel mixture over medium heat, stirring frequently, for about 10 minutes, before adding the basil and seasoning.

stewed bell peppers, tomatoes, and onions
peperonata

Just about every region of Italy has its own favorite pepper speciality, but this must be the best-known and most popular recipe.

SERVES 4

5 tbsp. olive oil

2 large onions, sliced thinly

1 garlic clove, chopped finely

3 red bell peppers, seeded and cut into strips

3 yellow bell peppers, seeded and cut into strips

12 tomatoes, peeled (see page 36) and chopped

salt

1 tbsp. white wine vinegar

1 Heat the olive oil in a heavy-bottom skillet. Add the onions, garlic, and bell peppers, and cook over low heat, stirring occasionally, for 15 minutes.

2 Add the tomatoes and season to taste with salt. Stir in the vinegar, cover, and let simmer for 30 minutes, until very tender. Serve immediately.

variation

For *Peperonata alla Romana*, stir in 1 tablespoon rinsed capers just before serving.

bell peppers and potatoes
peperoni e patate

In Italy, potatoes are often combined with other vegetables, rather than cooked as a separate accompaniment. Here, mixed bell peppers provide plenty of color and extra flavor, and fresh chili gives additional bite.

SERVES 4

1 fresh red chili, seeded

2 garlic cloves

bunch of fresh flat-leaf parsley

½ cup virgin olive oil

1 lb. waxy potatoes, sliced thinly

2 tbsp. hot water (optional)

1 lb. mixed red and orange bell peppers, seeded and diced

salt

1 Place the chili, garlic, and parsley on a cutting board and chop together until very fine and well mixed. Heat half the oil in a large, heavy-bottom skillet. Add half the chili mixture and cook over medium heat, stirring constantly, for 1 minute.

2 Add the potatoes, reduce the heat, and cook, turning frequently, for 15–20 minutes. Add the hot water if the potato slices start to stick.

3 Meanwhile, heat the remaining oil in another skillet, add the remaining chili mixture and cook over medium heat, stirring constantly, for 1 minute. Add the bell peppers and cook, stirring frequently, for 15–20 minutes, until tender.

4 Combine the potato and bell pepper mixtures in a large warmed serving bowl, season with salt, and serve immediately.

*cook's tip
If the potatoes are tender before the bell peppers are cooked, cover the pan with a lid to keep them warm.

Left *Winding streets of a typical traditional Tuscan village*

Overleaf *The dome of St. Peter's Church as dusk falls over Rome*

210

spinach and ricotta dumplings
gnocchi di spinaci e ricotta

These mouthwatering dumplings made with spinach and ricotta cheese are best served simply, coated in an herb butter and sprinkled with Parmesan cheese.

SERVES 4

2 lb. 4 oz. fresh spinach, coarse stalks removed

1 1/2 cups ricotta cheese

1 cup freshly grated Parmesan cheese

3 eggs, beaten lightly

pinch of freshly grated nutmeg

salt and pepper

generous 3/4 cup all-purpose flour, plus extra
  for dusting

for the herb butter

4 oz. unsalted butter

2 tbsp. chopped fresh oregano

2 tbsp. chopped fresh sage

1 Wash the spinach, then place it in a pan with just the water clinging to its leaves. Cover and cook over low heat for 6–8 minutes, until just wilted. Drain well and set aside to cool.

2 Squeeze or press out as much liquid as possible from the spinach,* then chop finely or process in a food processor or blender. Place the spinach in a bowl and add the ricotta, half the Parmesan, the eggs, and nutmeg, and season to taste with salt and pepper. Beat until thoroughly combined. Start by sifting in 3/4 cup of the flour and lightly work it into the mixture, adding more, if necessary, to make a workable mixture. Cover with plastic wrap and let chill for 1 hour.

3 With floured hands, break off small pieces of the mixture and roll them into walnut-size balls. Handle them as little as possible, because they are quite delicate. Lightly dust the dumplings with flour.

4 Bring a large pan of lightly salted water to a boil. Add the dumplings and cook for 2–3 minutes, until they rise to the surface. Remove them from the pan with a slotted spoon, drain well, and set aside.

5 Meanwhile, make the herb butter. Melt the butter in a large, heavy-bottom skillet. Add the oregano and sage and cook over low heat, stirring frequently, for 1 minute. Add the dumplings and toss gently for 1 minute to coat. Transfer to a warmed serving dish, sprinkle with the remaining Parmesan, and serve.

*cook's tip

A good way to remove the liquid from cooked spinach is to put it in a strainer and use a potato masher to press out the unwanted water.

basil dumplings
gnocchi alla genovese

In Italy, gnocchi are traditionally served as a primo or first course, but they can also make an unusual and delicious accompaniment to meat or fish.

3 cups milk

1³/₄ cups semolina

1 tbsp. finely chopped fresh basil leaves

4 sun-dried tomatoes in oil, drained and chopped finely

2 eggs, beaten lightly

2 oz. butter, plus extra for greasing

³/₄ cup freshly grated Parmesan cheese

salt and pepper

Tomato Sauce (see page 106), to serve

1 Pour the milk into a large pan and bring to just below boiling point. Sprinkle in the semolina, stirring constantly. Reduce the heat and let simmer gently for about 2 minutes, until thick and smooth. Remove the pan from the heat.

2 Stir in the basil, sun-dried tomatoes, eggs, half the butter, and half the Parmesan, and season to taste with salt and pepper. Stir well until all the ingredients are thoroughly incorporated, then pour into a shallow dish or baking sheet and level the surface. Set aside to cool, then chill for at least 1 hour, until set.

3 Lightly grease an ovenproof dish with butter. Using a lightly floured, plain, round cookie cutter, stamp out circles of the set semolina mixture. Place the trimmings in the bottom of the dish and top with the circles.

4 Melt the remaining butter and brush it over the semolina circles, then sprinkle with the remaining Parmesan. Bake in a preheated oven, 375°F, for 30–35 minutes, until golden. Serve immediately with tomato sauce.

porcini mushroom salad 215
insalata di funghi porcini

1 Thinly slice 1 lb. of the mushrooms and arrange them on a serving platter. Finely chop the remaining mushrooms and set aside (depending on their size, there may be only one or even only part of one remaining).

2 Put the olive oil and garlic in a heavy-bottom skillet and heat gently for 1 minute. Remove the garlic with a slotted spoon and discard.

3 Add the chopped mushrooms, season with salt, cover, and cook over low heat for 3–4 minutes. Remove the skillet from the heat and let cool slightly.

4 Transfer the warm mushroom mixture to a food processor or blender and process until smooth. Return the mixture to the skillet.

5 Set the skillet over low heat and gradually beat in the butter, a piece at a time, until it is fully incorporated. Do not let the mixture boil.

6 Meanwhile, place the platter of sliced mushrooms in a preheated oven, 250°F, to warm through slightly.

7 Stir the parsley into the sauce, pour it over the mushrooms, and serve warm.

variation
For a less indulgent dish, substitute other exotic mushrooms for the porcini.

This is the most gloriously extravagant salad, but worth every penny. Of course, Italian housekeeping budgets are helped by the fact that they are keen gatherers of wild mushrooms.

SERVES 4
1 lb. 2 oz. fresh porcini mushrooms
1 tbsp. extra virgin olive oil
1 garlic clove
salt
7 oz. unsalted butter, diced
1 tbsp. chopped fresh flat-leaf parsley

216

mozzarella salad with sun-dried tomatoes
mozzarella alla romana

Mozzarella is often included in salads, but this recipe from Rome is a more sophisticated version, as befits Italy's capital city.

SERVES 4

5 oz. sun-dried tomatoes in olive oil (drained weight), reserving the oil from the bottle

1 tbsp. fresh basil, shredded coarsely

1 tbsp. fresh flat-leaf parsley, chopped coarsely

1 tbsp. capers, rinsed

1 tbsp. balsamic vinegar

1 garlic clove, chopped coarsely

extra olive oil, if necessary

pepper

3$\frac{1}{2}$ oz. mixed salad greens, such as oak leaf lettuce, baby spinach, and arugula

1 lb. 2 oz. smoked mozzarella, sliced

1 Put the sun-dried tomatoes, basil, parsley, capers, vinegar, and garlic in a food processor or blender. Measure the oil from the sun-dried tomatoes jar and add in enough oil to make $\frac{2}{3}$ cup. Add it to the food processor or blender and process until smooth. Season to taste with pepper.

2 Divide the salad greens between 4 individual serving plates. Top with the slices of mozzarella and spoon the dressing over them. Serve immediately.

variation
Substitute Taleggio or a goat milk cheese for the mozzarella.

The residential area of Ponte Parione, Rome

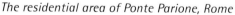

layered tomato salad
la panzanella

This is a popular salad throughout Italy and the perfect way of using up yesterday's bread. For the fullest flavor, use sun-ripened tomatoes.

SERVES 4

1 red onion, sliced thinly into rings

4 slices day-old bread

1 lb. tomatoes, sliced thinly

4 oz. mozzarella di bufala, sliced thinly

1 tbsp. shredded fresh basil

salt and pepper

$^1/_2$ cup extra virgin olive oil

3 tbsp. balsamic vinegar

4 tbsp. lemon juice

$^2/_3$ cup black olives, pitted and sliced thinly

1 Place the onion slices in a bowl and add cold water to cover. Set aside to soak for 10 minutes. Meanwhile, dip the slices of bread in a shallow dish of cold water, then squeeze out the excess. Place the bread in a serving dish.

2 Drain the onion slices and layer them on the bread with the tomatoes and mozzarella, sprinkling each layer with the basil and salt and pepper.

3 Pour over the olive oil, vinegar, and lemon juice, and sprinkle with the sliced olive. Cover and let chill for up to 8 hours before serving.

Typical hilltop Tuscan village

three-color salad
insalata tricolore

With the white mozzarella, red tomatoes, and green basil representing the colors of the Italian flag, this patriotic salad is served all over Italy and beyond.

SERVES 4

10 oz. mozzarella di bufala, drained and sliced thinly

8 plum tomatoes, sliced

salt and pepper

20 fresh basil leaves

¹/₂ cup extra virgin olive oil

1 Arrange the cheese and tomato slices on 4 individual serving plates and season to taste with salt. Set aside in a cool place for 30 minutes.

2 Sprinkle the basil leaves over the salad and drizzle with the olive oil. Season with pepper and serve immediately.

variations

There are dozens of variations to this salad. Add 24 pitted black olives and 5 drained and chopped anchovies before adding the basil in step 2. Alternatively, peel, halve, and pit 2 avocados. Cut the flesh crosswise into thin slices and arrange them over the salad before sprinkling with the basil in step 2. Thinly slice a small white and a small red onion and push out into rings. Arrange them on top of the salad before sprinkling with the basil in step 2.

artichoke and arugula salad   223
insalata di carciofi e rucola

This simple Tuscan salad is made from the small, tender artichokes of the early summer, but can also be made from the closely related cardoon. If using cardoons, cut off and discard the tough, outer stalks.

SERVES 4

8 baby globe artichokes

juice of 2 lemons

bunch of arugula

salt and pepper

½ cup extra virgin olive oil

4 oz. pecorino cheese

1 Break off the stems of the artichokes and cut off about 1 inch of the tops, depending on how young and small they are. Remove and discard any coarse outer leaves, leaving only the pale, tender inner leaves. Using a teaspoon, scoop out the chokes. Rub each artichoke with lemon juice as soon as it is prepared to prevent it from discoloring.

2 Thinly slice the artichokes and place in a salad bowl. Add the arugula, lemon juice, and olive oil, season to taste with salt and pepper, and toss well.

3 Using a swivel-blade vegetable peeler, thinly shave the pecorino over the salad, then serve immediately.

variation

If only larger artichokes are available, cook them in lightly salted boiling water for about 15 minutes, then refresh under cold running water before slicing.

Palace façade on the edge of Lake Como

pasta salad with charbroiled bell peppers
insalata di peperoni arrostiti

Traditionalists eat their pasta before the main course, and they eat it hot. Nevertheless, the booming tourist industry has brought some compromises in its wake—if only for those not fortunate enough to have been born in Italy.

SERVES 4

1 red bell pepper

1 orange bell pepper

10 oz. dried conchiglie

5 tbsp. extra virgin olive oil

2 tbsp. lemon juice

2 tbsp. Pesto (see page 36)

1 garlic clove

3 tbsp. shredded fresh basil leaves

salt and pepper

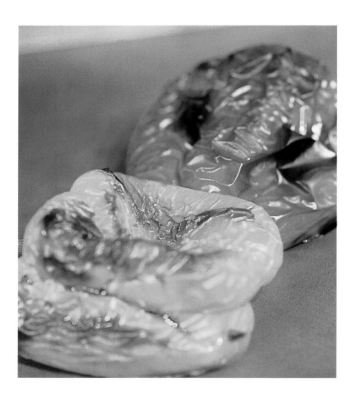

1 Put the whole bell peppers on a baking sheet and place under a preheated broiler, turning frequently, for 15 minutes, until charred all over. Remove with tongs and place in a bowl. Cover with crumpled paper towels and set aside.

2 Meanwhile, bring a large pan of lightly salted water to a boil. Add the pasta, bring back to a boil, and cook for 8–10 minutes, until tender but still firm to the bite.

3 Combine the olive oil, lemon juice, pesto, and garlic in a bowl, whisking well to mix. Drain the pasta, add it to the pesto mixture while still hot, and toss well. Set aside.

4 When the bell peppers are cool enough to handle, peel off the skins, then cut open and remove the seeds. Chop the flesh coarsely and add to the pasta with the basil. Season to taste with salt and pepper and toss well. Serve at room temperature.

variation

A more traditional salad, without the pasta, can be made in the same way. When the bell peppers have been under the broiler for 10 minutes, add 4 tomatoes and broil for an additional 5 minutes. Cover the bell peppers with paper towels, then peel and chop as in step 4. Peel and coarsely chop the tomatoes. Combine them with the dressing and garnish with black olives.

DESSERTS, CAKES, & DRINKS

228 Go to Rome for ice cream, to Florence for zabaglione, and to anywhere in the south of Italy for cheesecake and sticky, honey-flavored desserts. Italians don't prepare and cook desserts at home as a general rule, but if they want to celebrate a special occasion, they will do so in style. Finally, begin and end your meal with a delicious cocktail and superb coffee.

Everyday meals in Italy usually conclude with fresh fruit, possibly a choice of cheese, but on special occasions desserts are served. These are often elaborate confections bought from the local *pasticceria* or mouthwatering ice cream from the *gelateria*. One ice cream parlor in Rome claims to be the best in the world and boasts more than 200 different flavors.

However, there are Italian desserts within the scope of the home cook, that are still luxurious enough to be considered a special treat. *Tiramisù* (see page 238), a rich mixture of mascarpone cheese, coffee liqueur, chocolate, and cookies, has conquered half the world since its invention in the 1970s, not least because it is so easy to make. Making ice cream at home is time-consuming, but a *semifreddo* (see page 250) or a *granita* (see page 251) requires very little effort for surprisingly impressive results. Some of the traditional desserts do demand a little more skill and practice. The deceptively simple *zabaglione* (see page 239), for instance, must be beaten to precisely the right degree of creamy thickness for just the right length of time and then served immediately.

Many of the most delicious desserts come from southern Italy and from Sicily and Sardinia. This has

much to do with the ample fruit, nuts, and honey produced in these parts. *Cassata alla Siciliana* (see page 248), for example, is a sponge cake filled with a lavish blend of ricotta cheese, cherry liqueur, candied fruits, and chocolate, covered with heavy cream.

Home baking is not a major activity in the Italian kitchen because there are bakers and confectioners in every town and village. Most special baking is left to these professionals, but some cooks are happy to make the occasional cheesecake or chocolate loaf—a cross between a tea bread and a cake. However, there is no reason why eager cooks should not try their hand at baking a more specialist recipe such as *panforte*, the traditional Christmas cake from the Tuscan city of Sienna.

Italy is the world's largest wine producer, so it is hardly surprising that wine is drunk with most meals. There are several brands of Italian beer and a number of popular apéritifs for predinner drinks, as well as a selection of liqueurs to accompany an after-dinner espresso. Although there is no "national drink" in the way that Spain boasts its *sangría*, there are a number of internationally famous cocktails based on Italian ingredients. Italian vermouth features in numerous mixed drinks, even though the dry martini was not named after the famous brand but after its inventor, Martini de Anna de Toggia. The lovely crimson color of Campari, first manufactured by the Campari brothers in Milan in the nineteenth century, makes it a natural choice for cocktails, among them

One ice cream parlor in Rome claims to be the best in the world and boasts more than 200 different flavors

the elegant *negroni* (see page 253), the popular
Americano, and the more unusual Italian Stallion.
Another Lombardy liqueur, the bright yellow,
herb-flavored Galliano, features in a number
of contemporary cocktails, including the Harvey
Wallbanger. Amaretto, made from apricot kernels and
with a distinctive almond flavor, is also a favorite for
mixed drinks, including an entire family of Godfather,
Godmother, and several other relatives. Perhaps the

Above *Italian grapes make wines with a very distinctive
character. These bunches are drying on racks to
concentrate the fruit*

Overleaf *The domed interior of a Catholic cathedral in the
Vatican, Rome*

most delicious and least controversial way to serve it,
apart from as a straightforward liqueur, is to make
the Italian equivalent to Irish coffee, *espresso
amaretto* (see page 252).

232 ricotta cheesecake
crostata di ricotta

This melt-in-the-mouth cheesecake confirms my belief that all the best Italian desserts come from Sicily.

SERVES 6–8

for the pastry

1¹⁄₈ cups all-purpose flour, plus extra for dusting

3 tbsp. superfine sugar

salt

4 oz. unsalted butter, chilled and diced

1 egg yolk

for the filling

1 lb. ricotta cheese

¹⁄₂ cup heavy cream

2 eggs, plus 1 egg yolk

³⁄₈ cup superfine sugar

finely grated rind of 1 lemon

finely grated rind of 1 orange

equipment

9-in. tart pan with removable sides

1 To make the pastry, sift the flour with the sugar and a pinch of salt onto a counter and make a well in the center. Add the diced butter and egg yolk to the well and, using your fingertips, gradually work in the flour mixture until fully incorporated.

2 Gather up the dough and knead very lightly. Cut off about one-quarter, wrap in plastic wrap, and let chill in the refrigerator. Press the remaining dough into the base of the tart pan. Let chill for 30 minutes.

3 To make the filling, beat the ricotta with the cream, eggs and extra egg yolk, sugar, lemon rind, and orange rind. Cover with plastic wrap and set aside in the refrigerator until required.

4 Prick the base of the pastry shell all over with a fork. Line with foil, fill with pie weights, and bake blind in a preheated oven, 375°F, for 15 minutes.

5 Remove the pastry shell from the oven and take out the foil and pie weights. Stand the pan on a wire rack and set aside to cool.

6 Spoon the ricotta mixture into the pastry shell and level the surface. Roll out the reserved pastry on a lightly floured counter and cut it into strips. Arrange the strips over the filling in a lattice pattern, brushing the overlapping ends with water so that they stick.

7 Bake in the preheated oven, 375°F, for 30–35 minutes, until the top of the cheesecake is golden and the filling has set. Let cool on a wire rack before lifting off the side of the pan. Cut into wedges to serve.

1 Use a sharp knife to cut a slit in the rounded side of the shell of each chestnut, then place them in large pan. Add cold water to cover and bring to a boil. Boil for about 5 minutes, then remove with a slotted spoon. When cool enough to handle, but still warm, remove the shells. The inner skins should easily peel off at the same time.

2 Place the chestnuts in a clean, heavy-bottom pan, pour in the milk and add the bay leaf, cinnamon, and half the superfine sugar. Bring to a boil, stirring to dissolve the sugar. Reduce the heat, cover and let simmer gently, stirring occasionally, for about 40 minutes, until the chestnuts are very tender. Remove the pan from the heat and set aside to cool.

3 Remove and discard the bay leaf and cinnamon stick from the pan and transfer the contents to a food processor or blender. Process to a smooth purée. Alternatively, rub the mixture through a strainer with the back of a wooden spoon or purée in a mouli.

4 Beat the egg yolks with the remaining sugar until pale and fluffy and the whisk leaves a trail when lifted. Stir in the vanilla extract and rum, then gently fold in the chestnut purée.

5 Whip the cream in a separate bowl until it forms stiff peaks. Gently fold it into the chestnut mixture.

6 Lightly grease 6 ovenproof molds with butter and spoon the chestnut mixture into them. Stand the molds on a baking sheet and bake in a preheated oven, 350°F, for 10–15 minutes, until just set.

7 Set the molds aside to cool to room temperature before serving. Alternatively, cover and chill until required. To serve, turn out the molds onto individual plates and pipe a border of whipped cream around the base of each one.

chestnut mousse
spuma di castagne

235

Chestnuts feature prominently in Tuscan and Sardinian cooking and play an important, if more muted, role in Ligurian dishes.

SERVES 6

1 lb. sweet chestnuts

1¼ cups milk

1 bay leaf

2-in. cinnamon stick

generous ¾ cup superfine sugar

2 large eggs yolks

½ tsp. vanilla extract

4 tbsp. dark rum

⅔ cup heavy cream, plus extra to decorate

butter, for greasing

equipment

6 individual ovenproof molds or ramekins

236

mascarpone creams
crema di mascarpone

Rich and self-indulgent, these creamy desserts make the perfect end to a special-occasion meal.

SERVES 4

4 oz. amaretti cookies, crushed*

4 tbsp. amaretto or Maraschino

4 eggs, separated

generous 1/4 cup superfine sugar

1 cup mascarpone cheese

toasted slivered almonds, to decorate

1 Place the amaretti crumbs in a bowl, add the amaretto or Maraschino, and set aside to soak.

2 Meanwhile, beat the egg yolks with the superfine sugar until pale and thick. Fold in the mascarpone and soaked cookie crumbs.

3 Whisk the egg white in a separate, spotlessly clean bowl until stiff, then gently fold into the cheese mixture. Divide the mascarpone cream among 4 serving dishes and let chill for 1–2 hours. Sprinkle with toasted slivered almonds just before serving.

*cook's tip
The easiest way to make cookie crumbs is to place the cookies in a plastic bag and crush with a rolling pin.

238 creamy coffee and chocolate dessert
tiramisù

This rich and popular dessert is a relatively new invention, dating from the 1970s, but it quickly acquired global appeal. The name means "pick me up," but it isn't clear whether this is because it is so delicious that it acts as a tonic or so wonderful that you faint with delight on tasting it and have to be picked up off the floor!

SERVES 6

2 eggs, separated, plus 2 egg yolks

$^1\!/_2$ cup superfine sugar

1 tsp. vanilla extract

1 lb. 2 oz. mascarpone cheese

$^3\!/_4$ cup strong black coffee

$^1\!/_2$ cup Kahlúa, Tía Maria, rum, or brandy

24 ladyfingers

2 tbsp. unsweetened cocoa

2 tbsp. finely grated unsweetened chocolate

1 Whisk the 4 egg yolks with the sugar and vanilla extract in the top of a double boiler or in a heatproof bowl set over a pan of barely simmering water. When the mixture is pale and so thick that the whisk leaves a ribbon trail when lifted, remove the bowl from the heat and set aside to cool completely. Whisk the mixture occasionally to prevent a skin from forming.

2 When the egg yolk mixture is quite cool, whisk the mascarpone into the egg yolk mixture until thoroughly combined. With clean blades, whisk the egg whites in a separate, spotlessly clean bowl until they form soft peaks, then gently fold them into the mascarpone mixture with a figure-eight action.

3 Combine the coffee and liqueur, rum, or brandy in a shallow dish. Dip the ladyfingers into the mixture, one at a time, turning them quickly so that they absorb the liquid but do not fall apart. Arrange a layer of ladyfingers on the base of a serving dish.

4 Spoon about one-third of the mascarpone mixture on top, spreading it out evenly. Repeat the layers, dipping and turning the ladyfingers quickly in the coffee mixture. Finish with a layer of the mascarpone mixture and level the surface. Let chill for at least 1 hour or, preferably, overnight before serving.

5 Just before serving, sift the unsweetened cocoa evenly over the top of the dessert, then sprinkle with the grated chocolate.

foaming froth
zabaglione

This world-famous dessert gets its name from a Neapolitan dialect word, zapillare, which means to foam—and that sums up exactly the texture required. It is quite difficult to achieve the right texture of the egg yolks without their curdling, but it is certainly worth the effort.

SERVES 4

4 egg yolks

¹/₃ cup superfine sugar

5 tbsp. Marsala

amaretti cookies, to serve

1 Whisk the egg yolks with the sugar in a heatproof bowl or, if you have one, the top of a double boiler for about 1 minute.

2 Gently whisk in the Marsala. Set the bowl over a pan of barely simmering water or put the top of the double boiler on its bottom filled with barely simmering water, and whisk vigorously for 10–15 minutes, until thick, creamy and foamy.

3 Immediately pour into serving glasses and serve with amaretti cookies.

variations
You can use other wines, such as Champagne, Sauternes, or Madeira to flavor this dessert, or a liqueur, such as Chartreuse or Cointreau. You could also use a mixture of white wine and brandy, rum, or Maraschino.

almond cake 241
torta di mandorle

This rich cake is delicious served with fruit as a dessert or simply with a cup of coffee for a mid-morning snack. Using potato flour is the secret of its wonderful, soft texture.

SERVES 12–14

butter, for greasing

3 eggs, separated

⁵/₈ cup superfine sugar

³/₈ cup potato flour

1 cup almonds, blanched, peeled,
  and chopped finely

finely grated rind of 1 orange

generous ¹/₂ cup orange juice

salt

confectioners' sugar, for dusting

equipment

8-in. cake pan with removeable sides

1 Generously grease a round 8-inch cake pan. Beat the egg yolks with the sugar in a medium bowl until pale and thick and the mixture leaves a ribbon trail when the whisk is lifted. Stir in the potato flour, almonds, orange rind, and orange juice.

2 Whisk the egg whites with a pinch of salt in another bowl until stiff. Gently fold the whites into the egg yolk mixture.

3 Pour the mixture into the pan and bake in a preheated oven, 325°F, for 50–60 minutes, until golden and just firm to the touch. Turn out onto a wire rack to cool. Sift over a little confectioners' sugar to decorate before serving.

A typical Venetian backwater

242

tuscan christmas cake
panforte di siena

No celebration of Italian cooking can ignore this famous spicy Christmas cake.* It is extremely rich: keep your portions small.

SERVES 12–14

generous ³/₄ cup hazelnuts

generous ³/₄ cup almonds

¹/₂ cup candied peel

¹/₃ cup dried apricots,
  chopped finely

¹/₃ cup candied pineapple, chopped finely

grated rind of 1 orange

scant ¹/₂ cup all-purpose flour

2 tbsp. unsweetened cocoa

1 tsp. ground cinnamon

¹/₄ tsp. ground coriander

¹/₄ tsp. freshly grated nutmeg

¹/₄ tsp. ground cloves

generous ¹/₂ cup superfine sugar

¹/₂ cup honey

confectioners' sugar, to decorate

equipment

8-in. cake pan with removeable sides

1 Line the cake pan with parchment paper. Spread out the hazelnuts on a baking sheet and toast in a preheated oven, 350°F, for 10 minutes, until golden brown. Pour them onto a dish towel and rub off the skins. Meanwhile, spread out the almonds on a baking sheet and toast in the oven for 10 minutes, until golden. Watch carefully after 7 minutes because they can burn easily. Reduce the oven temperature to 300°F. Chop all the nuts and place in a large bowl.

2 Add the candied peel, apricots, pineapple, and orange rind to the nuts and mix well. Sift together the flour, unsweetened cocoa, cinnamon, coriander, nutmeg, and cloves into the bowl and mix well.

3 Put the sugar and honey into a pan and set over low heat, stirring, until the sugar has dissolved. Bring to a boil and cook for 5 minutes, until thickened and starting to darken. Stir the nut mixture into the pan and remove from the heat.

4 Spoon the mixture into the prepared cake pan and level the surface with the back of a damp spoon. Bake in the oven for 1 hour, then transfer to a wire rack to cool in the pan.

5 Carefully remove the cake from the pan and peel off the parchment paper. Just before serving, dredge the top with confectioners' sugar. Cut into thin wedges to serve.

*cook's tip
You can make this cake up to 2 weeks in advance. Store in an airtight container.

Overleaf *The main square, Piazza del Duomo, Milan*

246

stuffed peaches
pesche ripiene alla piemontese

Peaches grow throughout central and southern Italy—in fact this recipe comes from the Piedmont in the northwest.

SERVES 6

2 oz. unsalted butter, plus extra for greasing

6 large peaches*

¼ cup ground almonds

2 oz. amaretti cookies, crushed coarsely

1 tbsp. amaretto liqueur

½ tsp. grated lemon rind

1 tsp. unsweetened cocoa

2 tsp. confectioners' sugar

1 cup medium-dry white wine

1 Grease an ovenproof dish with butter. Cut the peaches in half, and remove and discard the pits. Widen the central cavity by cutting away and reserving some of the flesh in a bowl.

2 Add the almonds, amaretti, amaretto, lemon rind, and half the butter to the reserved peach flesh and mash with a fork. Fill the peach cavities with this mixture and place them in the dish.

3 Dot the peaches with the remaining butter and sprinkle with the unsweetened cocoa and confectioners' sugar. Pour the wine into the dish and bake in a preheated oven, 350°F, for 30 minutes, until golden. Serve immediately.

*cook's tip
Use white peaches if you can find them, because they have the sweetest and most succulent flavor. White or yellow, do make sure the peaches are really ripe.

marsala cherries

ciliege al marsala

This is a popular Venetian dish, made with Morello cherries—the variety most widely grown in Italy.

SERVES 4

⁵/₈ **cup superfine sugar**

thinly pared rind of 1 lemon

2-in. piece of cinnamon stick

1 cup water

1 cup Marsala

2 lb. Morello cherries, pitted

²/₃ **cup heavy cream**

1 Put the sugar, lemon rind, cinnamon stick, water, and Marsala in a heavy-bottom pan and bring to a boil, stirring constantly. Reduce the heat and let simmer for 5 minutes. Remove the cinnamon stick.

2 Add the Morello cherries, cover, and let simmer gently for 10 minutes. Using a slotted spoon, transfer the cherries to a bowl.

3 Return the pan to the heat and bring to a boil over high heat. Boil for 3–4 minutes, until thick and syrupy. Pour the syrup over the cherries and set aside to cool, then chill for at least 1 hour.

4 Whisk the cream until stiff peaks form. Divide the cherries and syrup between 4 individual dishes or glasses, top with the cream, and serve.

variation

Substitute a full-bodied red wine for the Marsala.

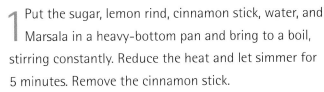

248

sicilian ice cream cake
cassata alla siciliana

Nowhere in Italy do they produce such lavish desserts as in Sicily. Although the term cassata, *which means "brick" and refers to the shape of the dessert, is usually applied to a luxurious ice cream, this glorious confection is an elaborate cake.*

SERVES 4

for the Genoa sponge cake
6 eggs, separated
1 cup superfine sugar
generous 1/2 cup self-rising flour
generous 1/2 cup cornstarch

for the filling
1 lb. 2 oz. ricotta cheese
1 cup superfine sugar
2 1/2 cups Maraschino* liqueur
3 oz. unsweetened chocolate
generous 1 cup mixed candied peel, diced
1 1/4 cups heavy cream

to decorate
glacé cherries, angelica, candied fruit, and
**   slivered almonds**

equipment
10-in. cake pan with removeable sides
2-lb. loaf pan

1 First, line the cake pan with parchment paper for the sponge cake.

2 Beat the egg yolks with the sugar until pale and frothy. In a separate, spotlessly clean bowl, whisk the whites until stiff peaks form. Gently fold the whites into the egg yolk mixture with a figure-eight action.

3 Sift together the flour and cornstarch into a bowl, then sift into the egg mixture and gently fold in. Pour the mixture into the cake pan and level the surface. Bake in a preheated oven, 350°F, for 30 minutes, until springy to the touch of a fingertip. Turn out onto a wire rack, remove the lining paper, and set aside to cool completely.

4 For the filling, combine the ricotta, sugar, and 1 3/4 cups of the Maraschino in a bowl, beating well. Chop the chocolate with a knife and stir it into the mixture with the candied fruit.

5 Cut the sponge cake into strips about 1/2 inch wide and use it to line the bottom and sides of the loaf pan. Set aside the remaining slices.

6 Spoon the ricotta mixture into the pan and level the surface. Cover the filling with the reserved strips of sponge cake. Drizzle the remaining Maraschino over the top, then chill overnight.

7 Run a round-bladed knife round the sides of the pan and turn out onto a serving plate. Whisk the heavy cream until stiff peaks form. Coat the top and sides of the cake with the cream and decorate with the cherries, angelica, candied fruit, and almonds.

*cook's tip
Maraschino is a sweet, colorless liqueur made from fermented bitter Maraschino cherries. If you prefer, you can use Cointreau.

250

chilled chocolate dessert
semifreddo al cioccolato

The range of Italian ice creams, sherbets, and water ices is breathtaking. This melt-in-the-mouth speciality is "semifrozen"—a cross between a mousse and an ice cream.

SERVES 4-6

1 cup mascarpone cheese
2 tbsp. finely ground coffee beans
¹/₄ cup confectioners' sugar
3 oz. unsweetened chocolate, grated finely
1¹/₂ cups heavy cream, plus extra to decorate
Marsala, to serve

1 Beat the mascarpone with the coffee and confectioners' sugar until thoroughly combined.

2 Set aside 4 teaspoons of the grated chocolate and stir the remainder into the cheese mixture with 5 tablespoons of the unwhipped cream.

3 Whisk the remaining cream until it forms soft peaks. Stir 1 tablespoon of the mascarpone mixture into the cream to slacken it, then fold the cream into the remaining mascarpone mixture with a figure-eight action.

4 Spoon the mixture into a freezerproof container and place in the freezer for about 3 hours.*

5 To serve, scoop the chocolate dessert into sundae glasses and drizzle with a little Marsala. Top with whipped cream and decorate with the reserved grated chocolate. Serve immediately.

*cook's tip
Do not freeze the mixture for too long or it will lose its texture.

lemon granita
granita al limone

*Halfway between a cold drink and a sherbet, a
refreshing granita with a citrus tang is the perfect
midsummer dessert. Alternatively, you can serve
it between courses as a palate cleanser.*

SERVES 4

2 cups water

generous ¹/₂ cup white granulated sugar

1 cup lemon juice

grated rind of 1 lemon

1 Heat the water in a heavy-bottom pan over
low heat. Add the sugar and stir until it has
completely dissolved. Bring to a boil, remove the pan
from the heat, and set the syrup aside to cool.

2 Stir the lemon juice and rind into the syrup. Pour
the mixture into a freezerproof container and place
in the freezer for 3–4 hours.

3 To serve, remove the container from the freezer
and dip the base into hot water. Turn out the
ice block and chop coarsely, then place in a food
processor* and process until it forms small crystals
(*granita* means "granular"). Spoon into sundae glasses
and serve immediately.

variations

Many different fruit syrups can be used to flavor
granitas—oranges, mandarins, pink grapefruit, or
mangoes. Simply substitute the juice in step 2. You
can add extra flavor with a splash of liqueur or include
herbs, such as lemon balm or elderflower, in the syrup
in step 1 (strain before pouring into the freezer
container). Coffee granita made with espresso coffee
instead of fruit juice, with or without a dash of liqueur,
is also delicious.

*cook's tip

An ordinary blender may not be sufficiently robust
to process the ice because it can damage the blades.
A good-quality food processor is recommended.

252

amaretto coffee
espresso amaretto

This is a lovely variation of Irish coffee. Amaretto is a deliciously sweet, almond-flavored liqueur made from apricot kernels. It is delicious drunk on its own, but it also forms the basis of a number of cocktails (see variations).

SERVES 1

2 tbsp. amaretto

1 cup hot black coffee

1 tbsp. heavy cream

1 Pour the amaretto into the cup of coffee and stir so the flavor mixes in well with the coffee.

2 Hold a teaspoon, rounded side upward, against the side of the cup with the tip just touching the surface of the coffee. Pour the cream over the back of the spoon so that it floats on top of the coffee. Serve immediately.

variations

For a Godfather, put ¼ cup Scotch whisky and 2 tablespoons amaretto into a chilled glass filled with ice cubes. Stir well and serve. For an Amaretto Rose, pour 2 tablespoons amaretto and 1 teaspoon lime cordial into a chilled glass filled with ice cubes. Stir well and fill with soda water or sparkling mineral water.

This aristocratic cocktail was invented by Count Negroni at the Bar Giacosa in Florence. Its color derives from Campari, the beautifully crimson aperitivo *with a bitter flavor, named after the brothers who first produced it in the nineteenth century and still made by the same family. Campari is often drunk simply with soda, but there are a number of other classic Campari cocktails (see variations).*

SERVES 1

ice cubes

2 tbsp. Campari

2 tbsp. dry gin

2 tbsp. Italian sweet vermouth

1 Put the ice cubes into a pitcher. Pour in the Campari, gin, and vermouth, and stir well.

2 Strain off the ice cubes into a cocktail glass and serve immediately.

variations

To make an Americano, put some ice cubes into a pitcher and pour in 2 tablespoons Campari and 2 tablespoons Italian sweet vermouth. Stir to mix, then strain into a tall glass. Fill with soda or sparkling mineral water and decorate with a slice of orange. To make an After One, put some ice cubes into a pitcher and pour in 2 tablespoons Campari, 2 tablespoons dry gin, 2 tablespoons Italian sweet vermouth, and 2 tablespoons Galliano. Stir to mix and strain into a cocktail glass.

index